Copyright

Be sure to check out Mike Riley's other books:

Hollywood Murders and Scandals: Tinsel Town After Dark

"In the late afternoon, her friends recalled, Monroe began to act strangely seeming to be heavily under the influence. She made statements to friend Peter Lawford that he should tell the President goodbye and tell himself goodbye."

More Hollywood Murders and Scandals: Tinsel Town After Dark

"At some point in the night Reeves and Lemmon began to argue. As Reeves headed upstairs to his bedroom, Lemmon would later tell officers that she shouted out that he would probably shoot himself."

Murders Unsolved: Cases That Have Baffled The Authorities For Years

"The body was wrapped in a plaid blanket, and placed inside a box that had once held a baby's bassinet purchased from J.C. Penney's. The boy was clean and dry, and recently groomed. However, he looked to be undernourished. Clumps of hair found on the body suggested he had been groomed after death."

Murders Unsolved Vol. 2: More Cases That Have Baffled the Authorities for Years

"McLeod first stopped at a payphone, but he didn't have any money, and so he drove to a nearby restaurant that was just opening. They didn't have a phone, but the owner gave him money to go back and use the payphone. He drove back and called the Sarasota police. Initially he was told he had to call the county Sheriff, but he responded that he didn't have any more money for more calls and then said, "They're all dead.""

America's Early Serial Killers: Five Cases of Frontier Madness

"We tend to think of those early settlers as hard working, decent people only looking for religious freedom and better opportunities for their families. However, even during those times, people existed who were depraved, evil and mentally ill. These are some of their stories."

Lost and Missing: True Stories of People Gone Missing and Never Found

"Police launched a massive search, reaching miles away from where the children were last seen in all directions. However, no evidence or any of their belongings were ever found. Even if three children could have been swept out to sea unnoticed on a crowded beach, what happened to their towels, clothes, and other items?"

Lost and Missing Vol. 2: More True Stories of People Gone Missing and Never Found

"Interestingly, it was discovered that the same day of the three women's disappearance, a concrete foundation was being poured at a hospital nearby. It would have perhaps been an ideal place to dispose of three bodies, but there is no evidence to support any such claim. It's rumoured that ground-penetrating radar discovered three anomalies in the set concrete, but it has never been dug up."

Table of Contents

Introduction

The worst thing most people can imagine is to have a loved one taken from them. All over the world, since the beginning of time people have taken each other's lives. It's called Murder. The word "murder" comes from the Middle English word mordre. It means to take a life in secret or unlawfully.

In the past, even with the diligent attempts and the best resources available to the authorities, many crimes including murders were never solved. In some cases the detective work was less than adequate and vital clues slipped through the fingers of those who could have solved the case earlier. Also, typically two detectives were assigned to solve each case and they were responsible for all of the components required to bring a criminal to court.

As technology has improved and become ever increasingly sophisticated, some crimes that were long ago considered "cold cases" have been reexamined and actually solved! Many of them have been solved through the use of DNA matching. Some others because of guilt where people can't keep their secret any longer and some just plain old good detective work.

The FBI has two key components that provide support to police departments requiring assistance in solving violent crimes. The Behavioral Analysis Unit (BAU) uses behavioral sciences and has elevated the level of sophistication involved in solving violent crimes.

The Violent Criminal Apprehension Program (ViCAP), is the largest information repository for investigation of major violent crimes in the US. It allows law enforcement agencies to identify patterns of violent crimes. ViCAP has been in use for over 25 years.

Please enjoy the following stories of cold cases that have finally been solved. There are cases that were decades old before they were solved and some more recent. The thing they have in common is that the perpetrator or perpetrators have finally been identified, and if possible, punished for their crimes.

The families and friends of the victims can have some sense of closure to their tragedies and with hope live the rest of their lives in peace.

The Oldest Solved Murder In American History

Victim: Maria Ridulph
Location: Sycamore, Illinois
Suspect: John Tessier
Date of Crime: December 3, 1957
Date of Conviction: September 14, 2012

Backstory:

Maria Ridulph was the youngest of four children born to Michael and Frances Ridulph. Born on March 12, 1950, she grew up with two older sisters and one older brother in Sycamore, Illinois, a farming community of seven thousand.

Ridulph's father worked in one of the few factories in the area. Her mother was a stay at home mom. In 1957, Ridulph was in the second grade. Just 3' 8" tall, she did very well at school, gaining a place as an honor student. She also had awards for perfect attendance at Sunday school at her family's church.

Her mother described her as "high strung" and "...a nervous girl". She claimed that Ridulph was very loud when upset, and also afraid of the dark. Did these tendencies ultimately lead to her demise?

On The Day In Question:

Tuesday December 3, 1957 was an ordinary day in the Ridulph household. Ridulph had attended school that day, and had her best friend, Kathy Sigman, over to play in the afternoon.

After each girl had eaten dinner at their own house, Ridulph pleaded with her parents to allow her to go outside again. The first snow flurries of the season had started and she was keen to go outside and play in the snow. Ridulph wanted to meet her friend Sigman again at the intersection of Center Cross Street and Archie Place, a favorite hangout.

Interestingly, since Halloween someone had been scrawling obscene messages on a tree at the intersection, using chalk. However, if Ridulph's parents knew about the messages, it did not prevent them from giving her permission to play there.

Excited to go out, Ridulph called Sigman, and after she also had permission, they met on the corner of the intersection. They played there for a while, ducking between the tree and a street pole, 'avoiding' headlights from oncoming cars. In the small mid-western town in the 1950's, everyone knew everyone else, and it was seen as perfectly safe for the two girls to play outside alone.

According to a later description from Sigman, a man in his early twenties approached the girls on the corner. She described him as being tall, with a slender chin. He had light colored hair done in the famous 'ducktail' style of the era, and was wearing a colorful sweater. He also had a gap in his front teeth. The man spoke to the girls, telling them his name was "Johnny", and asking if they liked dolls. He told the girls that he was twenty-four years old and unmarried.

Ridulph went into her house just three doors down and retrieved a doll to show Johnny, and then the man gave her a piggyback ride. While Ridulph was retrieving the doll, Sigman much later reported that Johnny asked her if she wanted to go for a walk around the block, or on a trip in a car, truck or bus. She told him no. Johnny then told her she was pretty, but looking back on the scene, an older Sigman says she could sense that he had his sights set on Maria.

When Ridulph returned, Sigman felt cold and so went to her own house to get her mittens, and when she returned both Ridulph and Johnny had disappeared.

Sigman immediately went into Ridulph's home and told Ridulph's parents that she couldn't find her. Initially thinking that she was hiding, they sent her eleven-year-old brother out to find her. He found no trace of his little sister, but he did find her doll lying abandoned next to a neighbor's garage. It was then that a sense of foreboding first came over him.

After searching for an hour and coming up empty handed, Ridulph's parents called the police. Police and armed civilians were searching for Ridulph within an hour. They searched the entire neighborhood, including opening cellars and looking inside cars.

Investigation:
The initial searches failed to find Ridulph, and the case was starting to gain national attention. It even caught the attention of President Eisenhower, and the FBI arrived within two days to assist with the search. Back in 1957, there was nothing like an Amber Alert or milk carton photos of missing children. The kidnapping of a small girl at that time shattered long held beliefs of decency and safety. The case was huge news.

Police searched every car entering or leaving the small town. Citizens were urged to leave outside lights on, and to immediately report anything suspicious. Roadblocks were set up, and every single house in the town was searched. They also searched known hangouts, storm drains, public bus stations, and even set off dynamite in a quarry. They never found a thing.

Reporters from all over the country arrived in the small town, traveling from as far as New York and Chicago. The director of the FBI, then J. Edgar Hoover, demanded daily updates from the investigation.

As the only witness, and for fear of her own safety, Sigman was put into protective custody. Both the local police and the FBI were concerned that the kidnapper would come back and take or harm her to prevent her from identifying him.

Law enforcement had Sigman look repeatedly at mug shots of people who resembled the man she described, but she never picked anyone out. The police also closely examined anyone in the town and the surrounding county that had a prior conviction for child molestation. However, this too revealed no leads.

When she had been missing for three weeks, Ridulph's tearful parents appeared on TV, pleading for their daughter's release and for her to return home unharmed. However, there would be little further development in the case for four months, until the fateful day of April 26, 1958.

On that day, a retired farmer named Frank Sitar was searching for mushrooms with his wife, when they stumbled across a terrible find. Under a partially fallen tree they discovered the skeletal remains of a small child. The skeleton was still fully clothed, minus shoes. Based on the remaining clothing and dental records the body was identified as Maria Ridulph.

The body was found over one hundred and twenty miles from her hometown, but still within the State of Illinois. Because the case did not cross state lines, the FBI withdrew at this point.

It seems strange to us in this day and age, but perhaps the 1950's were a more innocent time, as the coroner did not take a single photo of the crime scene, worried that the photos would be leaked to the newspapers. These days, no doubt multiple photos would be taken and may appear online. It is unknown whether the lack of crime scene photos had an influence on eventually solving the case.

Decomposition, plus damage to the remains from animals, prevented a definitive cause of death, though the autopsy revealed injuries to Ridulph's chest and throat, indicative of being stabbed.

Though her body had been found, no further leads of note were discovered. DNA testing did not exist, and there were no further witnesses beyond eight-year-old Sigman's description of the man they had been playing with. No one had seen him actually take Ridulph. Much of the physical evidence, such as Ridulph's doll that the killer handled, was eventually lost to the passage of time.

The world moved on, and the case of Ridulph's murder would lay unsolved for fifty-four years.

Current Status:
In 1994, a woman named Eileen Tessier was on her deathbed, and as a dying confession she told her daughters that she had provided her son with a false alibi some thirty-six years earlier.

Tessier's son, John Tessier, had changed his name to Jack Daniel McCullough. His half-sister, Janet Tessier, reported him to the Illinois State Police. His other sister, Mary Pat, was also in the room, but it has been reported that even the two sisters cannot exactly agree on what their mother said.

Since the confession, Janet Tessier had been trying to find a law enforcement agency that would take another look at the case based on her information.

Two previous attempts to contact law enforcement had been dismissed. Tessier reports that she was told the deathbed confession was inadmissible in a court of law, and that there was no longer any physical evidence that could be used. It would be another fourteen years before the case would break wide open.

In 2008, the Illinois State Police took on the case, and started an extensive background check into Tessier, and most importantly, his alibi. Using a picture of him from 1957, investigators found an old girlfriend of Tessier's.

When contacted, she reported that she had found an unused train ticket dated December 1957. The ticket was to Rockford, Illinois. Tessier's alibi was that he was traveling to Rockford on December 3rd for a medical exam to enlist in the US Air Force. Police realized the ticket had never been used and it was highly likely that Tessier had in fact been in town the day Ridulph disappeared.

They established a timeline of that day, and realized that it was possible that Tessier had enough time to take Ridulph, kill her, drive her body to where it was eventually found, and then return to town. Investigators were also able to locate childhood friends of Tessier's that placed him in town on that day.

Police found Sigman, now an adult, and showed her a lineup of six photos of teenagers, all of whom had lived in Sycamore in 1957. For the first time, it included a photo of Tessier as he had appeared then. It was more than fifty years later, but she immediately identified him as "Johnny".

Another three years passed and in 2011 Tessier was finally brought in for questioning. He had been found living in a retirement community, working there as a security guard. Ironically, he had for the most part lived a law-abiding life. After rising to the rank of captain in the military, he retired from active duty and became a police officer in the state of Washington.

However, in 1971 he was fired and charged with sexual assault after a fourteen-year-old runaway he had taken into his home accused him of touching her and forcing her to have sex with him.

Despite the allegations, he was allowed to plead guilty to simple assault, a misdemeanor. It was after the conviction that he changed his name, allegedly to honor his mother with her surname. Many however believe it was to avoid further suspicion landing on him for other crimes.

Because of his own professional experience working in law enforcement and the military, Illinois State Police decided to bring in a professional interrogator to interview Tessier. Investigators reported that during the interview he was calm and co-operative.

However when the questions turned to his involvement in Ridulph's murder, he is reported to have become evasive and aggressive. He refused to answer any further questions, and was arrested for Ridulph's kidnapping and murder in July 2011.

That same month, investigators exhumed and examined Ridulph's body, but no new evidence was found.

Wary of going to trial with only circumstantial evidence, the prosecution decided to first move forward with a case against Tessier for another sexual assault he had allegedly been involved in – the gang rape of his own sister.

With the same prosecutor taking the lead in both cases, the first went to trial in the spring of 2012. Evidence included police reports about Tessier's interest in young girls. Witnesses included his sister, other siblings, and the girl he was accused of sexually assaulting when he was a police officer in 1971.

The defense argued that his sister's story could not be corroborated. She had not told her story to anyone else before Tessier had been arrested for Ridulph's murder, and there was no remaining physical evidence to suggest rape. After so many years it was highly unlikely that there would be any physical evidence to collect, whether the act was consensual or not.

Tessier did not take the stand, and after just one day of deliberations the judge dismissed the case, saying that the prosecution had failed to prove that a rape had occurred.

Undeterred, in September of 2012 the same prosecutor took Tessier to trial for Ridulph's murder. Their argument was that at first he meant to only kidnap Ridulph, but then ended up killing her instead. Evidence included the original autopsy reports. Though, perhaps learning from the first trial, as there was no physical evidence of sexual assault, they did not raise it at all in this trial.

The defense's argument was similar, there was no physical evidence linking Tessier to the crimes, and law enforcement was unable to prove he had even been in the area on the day in question. They also accused the prosecution of being under pressure to close the case after the alleged deathbed confession from Tessier's mother became publically known.

There were many witnesses for the prosecution, including Ridulph's childhood friend from that fateful day half a century ago, Kathy Sigman. Also testifying for the prosecution were both Ridulph's and Tessier's siblings, law enforcement from several states, and another childhood friend of Ridulph's, who testified she had been separately approached by "Johnny" and given a piggy-back ride.

Additionally, the prosecution had three inmates who had been in jail with Tessier testify that he had admitted to them that he killed Ridulph. However, their stories were inconsistent, with cause of death ranging from strangulation with wire to smothering. Was there any truth in their testimony, or were they simply in it for themselves or for reasons unknown?

Again, Tessier did not take the stand in his own defense. This time however, the outcome was different. On September 14, 2012, he was convicted of both the kidnapping and murder of Ridulph. Already seventy-three when convicted, he was given a life sentence with the possibility of parole. Unfortunately Ridulph's parents died in 1999 and 2007 and did not live to see the guilty verdict handed down in their daughter's murder.

It's now known that Tessier, was among the original list of suspects, and had even been questioned by the FBI during the first investigation. However after he had been interviewed and had an alibi given by his parents for December 3rd, law enforcement did not have Sigman try to identify him.

This was largely in part because he had been given a polygraph by law enforcement, and he passed. Back then, it was believed impossible for a guilty man to pass the test. In modern times we know that there are several ways that lie detector tests can be manipulated and fooled.

The discovery of the true killer was also hampered by the fact that most local law enforcement believed it impossible that such a terrible crime could have been committed by someone who lived in their town. They believed that it had to be the work of a trucker or someone else just passing through. Only the FBI was looking at local suspects.

Was Ridulph killed immediately after her abduction, or would she perhaps still be alive today had police shown Tessier's photo to Sigman when Ridulph was first abducted? There are many moments in this case that would likely be vastly different had they occurred today.

Ridulph's childhood friend who went home for her mittens when Ridulph was taken says that Tessier also stole her childhood. As well as living with survivor guilt, for the rest of her childhood many parents would not allow their children to ever play with her, afraid that the then unknown killer would come back for Sigman and take their child too.

Even after her family moved to another part of town she could not escape. As a teen, the mother of a young man interested in asking her out told him in front of Sigman "Don't you know who she is? ...can't you find someone else?" The young man however was not deterred, and he would marry Sigman in 1969.

Tessier requested a new trial and was denied at sentencing. However his appeal continues today.

It is believed that the murder of Maria Ridulph is the oldest unsolved murder that eventually resulted in an arrest and conviction in the history of America.

Victims: Cheryl Kay Miller and Pam Jackson
Location: Vermillion, Clay County, South Dakota
Suspect: David Lykken
Date Disappeared: May 29, 1971
Date Solved: September 2013

Backstory:
Vermillion, South Dakota is located at the very southeast corner of the state, very near the Iowa and Nebraska borders. Today it is the home of the University of South Dakota and has a population of around 11,000 people. In 1971, its population was just around 1,000.

Cheryl Kay Miller was born on November 16, 1953 to parents Helen and Melvin Miller. She had three sisters, Linda, Dawn and Rita, just 9 when Cheryl disappeared, and one brother Allen.

After her parents split up she went to live with her grandparents, Nick and Pearl Jensen. Grandmother Pearl was very ill and near death when the tragedy occurred.

Pamela Jackson was born on January 24, 1954 to parents Adele and Oscar. Her family consisted of brothers Darryl and Jerry and sister Kay. Pam was the youngest. The family had a farm where Pam was involved in 4H and other rural activities.

Miller was a tall girl at approximately 5' 10", and weighed 130 pounds. She had blonde hair and blue eyes. Jackson was a brunette with hazel eyes, and stood shorter at approximately 5' 8" and weighed 150 pounds.

Both girls were juniors at Vermillion High School and 17 years old. They both worked at Vermillion Hospital. They had plans to go to California upon graduation with Cheryl, also known as Sherri, becoming a dress designer and Pam a dressmaker.

On The Day In Question:
On the day of their disappearance in May of 1971, they had been driving down rural roads, traveling to attend a party in a gravel pit at a lake, about fifteen miles south of Beresford, South Dakota. The town was about 30 miles away from Vermillion.

Earlier that day the girls had both visited Miller's grandmother, who was in the hospital. They then stopped to talk to some boys outside a church. A fellow attendee of the church, David Lykken, was a friend of Jackson's. He did not attend the same school as the girls, but the party the girls were attending was only a few miles from Lykken's home.

Miller and Jackson asked the boys for directions, and then started to follow them to the party at the gravel pit. The girls were driving a 1960 beige Studebaker Lark. At one point the boys lost track of the girls in their review mirror, and continued on to the party.

Miller and Jackson never arrived.

Investigation:
A friend and classmate, LuAnn Sorensen-Denke had also planned to follow Miller and Jackson's car to the party. At the last minute however she decided that the roads were too dangerous and turned around. However, she has reported that Jackson knew those roads very well, and she was confident that her friends would have been fine.

Sorensen-Denke, along with other classmates, has raised concerns about how the case was initially investigated. They believe there was a delay in starting the investigation by the police. One of the boys in the car has reported that he was never interviewed in relation to the girls' disappearance.

For years after their disappearance he often wondered what happened to them. He claims it should have been easy to find the girls. The only thing between their last sight of the girls in their rear view mirror and noticing they were gone was a creek.

There were also rumors from some others who knew the girls that they had run off to live in a hippie commune, or had driven off to travel to California. However those who were closest to the pair have disputed these claims. A friend described them both as "...very family oriented, very church oriented."

The area was extensively searched, but nothing was found.

The disappearance of Miller and Jackson would remain a mystery for another forty years. In September 2013 a fisherman was walking near Brule Creek in Beresford, South Dakota. He saw the wheels of a car sticking out of the water, very close to a bridge. The gravel pit the girls had been traveling to was less than a half mile away.

The car was pulled from the creek. It was clear that it had been there for a very long time, and was badly damaged. However the license plate could still be read, and it matched the car the girls had been driving. The skeletal remains of two women were found in the car.

Current Status:
The case of the disappearance of Miller and Jackson was one of the first cases handled by South Dakota's Cold Case Unit when it was formed in 2004.

The bridge near where the car was eventually found had been inspected every two years for at least the last twenty years. How did authorities miss finding the car lying there all that time? It's been suggested that if just an axel or single wheel re-emerged that it may have been ignored by anyone who spotted it.

It was a relatively common practice back in earlier times for landowners to discard old farm equipment and vehicles in public waters. They were said to help prevent erosion along the banks.

The week before the car was found there had been a large amount of rainfall, which caused flooding in the creek. Perhaps it was enough to dislodge things long hidden from view.

Jackson's friend David Lykken ended up leading a life on the dark side. He was almost tried for the kidnapping and murder of both Miller and Jackson, after being implicated by a jailhouse snitch.

His own sister also recalled memories under hypnosis of seeing the girls' car at their parent's farm. The trial was scheduled, but prosecutors dropped the charges after it was discovered that the snitch lied.

Lykken however was already in prison for convictions on multiple unrelated charges of rape and burglary. For those crimes he was sentenced to more than two hundred years in jail. Many still believe that he was at least involved in Miller and Jackson's disappearance. If he was, at least justice has been partially served.

The current theory from investigators is that Miller and Jackson were killed when their car accidently left the gravel road and drove into the creek. When the car was discovered, it was still in third gear, the keys were in the ignition, and the headlights were set to on.

Personal items for both young women were found in the car. There was no evidence of alcohol. One tire was damaged. Did they suffer a blowout and veer off the road? When the accident happened, the bridge was still new. Perhaps it confused Jackson, despite her being familiar with the roads in the area.

Even though we now know the final resting place of the girls, we may never know how their car ended up in the creek. Jackson's father never gave up hope of finding his daughter, and was still searching for her to his dying day. Tragically, he passed away barely a week before the car and his daughter's remains were found.

The 100th Denver Cold Case

Victim: Patricia Beard
Location: Denver, Colorado
Suspect: Hector Bencomo-Hinojos
Date of Crime: March 27, 1981
Date Identified: July 11, 2013

Backstory:
Very little is known about the victim in this case, Patricia Beard. She was born on January 1, 1949. Beard, who was thirty-two when she was murdered, was mentally disabled. She lived in a studio apartment on East 11th Avenue in Denver, Colorado.

On The Day In Question:
Just before 3:00pm on March 27, 1981, Beard was found lying dead inside her apartment. She had been left lying face up on her bed. Her robe was open, and her panties were left around her ankle on her right leg. Her slip had been pushed up over her genitals, and a used tampon was found near the body.

Friends and family had not seen her for several days prior to the discovery of her body. A family member who went to check on her discovered her partially clothed body lying on the bed.

Investigation:
The autopsy reported a laceration on her left breast. She also had a bone fracture and hemorrhaged extensively along her neck. She had been strangled. The official cause of death was asphyxiation. DNA evidence was taken from Beard's body.

Investigating officers believe that the killer entered the home through a window. They also discovered a brick on the exterior of the building they believe was used as a foothold.

Despite investigator's efforts, the murder of Patricia Beard would remain unsolved for twenty years.

Many years after Beard's murder, as part of the Denver District Attorney's office new focus on cold cases, the DNA evidence from Beard's case was entered into an FBI database, and a match was found. The database gave the name of Hector Bencomo-Hinojos, a man who was fifty-three years old, and who was currently incarcerated in a federal prison for an unrelated crime.

Before he was informed his DNA had matched, Bencomo-Hinojos claimed that he did not recognize Beard when shown a photo, and also claimed he had never had sex with an African-American woman. Amazingly, even when informed of the DNA match, his denials continued.

Investigators also tracked down Bencomo-Hinojos' wife. She told investigators that her husband was a physically abusive man. She told police that he would slap her across the face if she didn't complete the ironing by the time he got home. She also reported that multiple times he had arrived home with what she thought were stolen goods.

Bencomo-Hinojos claimed he was looking after the things for friends, but perhaps they were evidence of other illegal activities, or even trophies taken from victims' apartments?

Current Status:
As a result of the DNA match, Bencomo-Hinojos now faces extradition to stand trial for Beard's rape and murder.

The case was the 100th cold case handled by the Denver District Attorney's Office. The office has made solving cold cases a special mission. No other law enforcement agency in the world has solved more cold cases.

Victims: Yolanda Sapp, Nickie Lowe, and Kathleen Brisbois
Location: Spokane, Washington
Suspect: Douglas/Donna Perry
Date of Crimes: Spring of 1990
Date of Identification: September 2012

Backstory:
It was spring of 1990, and in Spokane, Washington multiple murder cases had caught investigators' eyes. Over a time period of four months, three women were murdered: Yolanda Sapp (26), Nickie Lowe (34) and Kathleen Brisbois (38).

All three women were prostitutes and were also known to use drugs. Three bodies found in the same area within such a short timespan had the police worried. Was there a serial killer on the loose?

On The Days In Question:
The body of Yolanda Sapp was the first to be found, February 22, 1990. She was found in the 4100 block of East Upriver Drive.

On March 25, Nickie Lowe's body was found in the 3200 block of East South Riverton, lying underneath the Greene Street Bridge.

Brisbois' body was the last to be discovered on May 15, discovered on the west side of the Spokane River, near Trent and Pines. Each had been killed with a .22 caliber gun.

Investigation:
The three murder cases caught investigator's attention, as it was unusual to have so many victims in such a short

period of time. From the beginning, investigators believed that they were seeing the work of a serial killer.

The case went cold, but it never left investigator's minds. In 2005, Brisbois' murder case was assigned to Sheriff's Detective James Dresback.

At the time of the murders the ability to test DNA evidence was not as advanced as it is now, but evidence was still collected from the bodies of the three women.

By 2009 the technology for testing of DNA evidence had advanced to the point that detectives resubmitted the evidence. A lab scientist quickly alerted Dresback that a sample from under Brisbois' nail had been successful in generating a full profile of a male. However the DNA had not matched anyone in the federal criminal database.

It would not be until September 2012 that the case would break wide open. A Washington State Patrol Crime Laboratory technician was testing the DNA of Douglas Perry, who had been arrested back in March in Spokane.

He was currently in federal custody in Carswell, Texas. He had been arrested after a retired detective saw Perry buying ammunition and a pistol magazine at a White Elephant store in the Spokane Valley. The detective knew that Perry was a convicted felon and was not allowed to have any firearms in his possession.

Then came the kicker. Douglas Perry was no longer Douglas Perry. In 2000, after the murders of the three women, Perry had traveled to Bangkok, Thailand, where he had undergone gender reassignment surgery. Now calling herself Donna Perry, Perry lived as a woman.

Perry's home was searched, and it was there that federal agents found more than twelve other firearms, and 12,000 rounds of ammunition. They also found a box of women's panties in the closet, in sizes that were too small to fit Perry. Right away, ATF Special Agent Todd Smith thought that this was a classic case of 'trophies' taken from victims.

Then, a second discovery would confirm Perry's involvement for investigators. In October, latent fingerprints were found on items that had been recovered from a dumpster in Lowe's murder case. When lifted and compared to Perry's, there was a match. Investigators could now link Perry to both women's deaths.

As well as his alleged involvement in the murders of Sapp, Lowe, and Brisbois, Perry's history includes convictions for reckless endangerment, assault, patronizing a prostitute, and possession of a pipe bomb and firearms.

Inmates from when Perry had been incarcerated also said that Perry had acted very strangely in jail. He had talked about taking prostitutes home and feeding them. A cellmate of Perry's claimed that he had confessed to him that he had killed a total of nine women, all prostitutes. Perhaps linked to his reasons for undergoing gender reassignment surgery, Perry allegedly killed the victims because they had the ability to have children but were "wasting it on pond scum".

When Perry appeared in court, she claimed that it was her male persona who had committed the murders, and the woman who she was now was innocent. She claimed that becoming a woman stopped the murders, and that gender treatments were a cure for men who were violent towards women. She claims to be unaware if Douglas Perry ever killed anyone.

Current Status:
The case against Perry remains ongoing.

Originally, investigators believed that the three women were likely victims of the serial killer Robert L. Yates, who was convicted of killing thirteen women in Spokane County, and two others in Pierce County, the majority of which were killed in the late 1990's. Yates was convicted of those murders and remains on death row.

An Inmate Points The Way

Victim: Rayna L. Rison
Location: La Porte, Indiana
Suspect: Jason Tibbs
Date of Crime: March 26, 1993
Date of Conviction: November 7, 2014

Backstory:
Rayna L. Rison was born in La Porte, Indiana on May 6, 1976 to Ben and Karen Rison. She had two sisters, Lori, and Wendy who was one year younger than Rayna.

In 1993, Rayna Rison was just sixteen years old. She worked at the Pine Lake Animal Hospital in La Porte, Indiana, and was a junior in high school.

La Porte is in the northern tip of Indiana with a current population of a little over 22,000 and was about that size in 1993.

On The Day In Question:
On March 26, 1993, Rison was working at the Animal Hospital. Her boyfriend, Matt Elser, arrived at her house at 5:15pm to wait for her. She was supposed to return home after finishing work at 6:00pm, and the couple would then go to dinner and a movie.

When Rison didn't return home by 7:00pm, Elser drove to the animal hospital. Her car was not in the parking lot. Rison's father, Ben Rison, then reported her missing. She would not be seen alive again.

Investigation:
The day after Rison was reported missing, investigators located her car in a rural area, several miles north of her hometown. Witnesses had reported seeing it in that location as early as 6:45pm the night before.

Police found a varsity athletic jacket hanging in a tree about six miles south of where Rison's car was found. It belonged to Jason Tibbs, an ex-boyfriend of Rison's. A ring belonging to Tibbs was also found in Rison's car.

Several witnesses reported two men in a car hanging around near Rison's work, but the lead did not result in any further information. Rison remained missing.

A month later, on April 27, 1993, a fisherman found Rison's body in a pond near Range Road, La Porte County.

Following an autopsy, Rison's death was ruled a homicide. The cause of death was 'asphyxia due to cervical compression'. She had been strangled.

Despite investigators efforts, the case remained unsolved.

Early in the case, some believed that Rison was a victim of serial killer Larry DeWayne Hall. Hall is serving a life sentence from a federal charge of kidnapping. However, he was never charged in relation to Rison's case.

In May of 1998, Rison's brother-in-law, Raymond McCarty, was charged and indicted with her murder. He spent fifteen months in jail awaiting trial, where he pled not guilty. When a new county prosecutor was elected, he dropped the charges against McCarty in August of 1999, citing lack of evidence.

McCarty had a sexual relationship with Rison when she was just thirteen years old, and she became pregnant. He received a three year suspended sentence in 1990. He had visited Rison at her job on the day she went missing.

In March of 2008, police received a tip regarding a friend of Jason Tibbs. An inmate at the Wabash Valley Correctional Facility, Rickey Hammons, told police to focus on Tibbs, who was an ex-boyfriend of Rison's at the time of her death. He also told police to look for his own sister's ex, a man named Eric Freeman.

Hammons told police that in March of 1993, he had been in his family's barn preparing a marijuana joint when both Freeman and Tibbs pulled up in his sister's car. When Freeman opened the trunk, Hammon saw someone lying in it, face up. At the time, he claimed he did not know it was Rison, but recognized her after seeing her photo in the paper.

Police spoke to Freeman, but he denied Hammon's account. It would then take six more years for investigators to gather any further information from Freeman. In July of 2013, Freeman was offered immunity from prosecution in Rison's case. He then started talking.

Freeman admitted that he drove Tibbs to Rison's workplace on that day. He then witnessed an argument between the pair. He drove both Rison and Tibbs to another location, where they got out of the car and continued to argue. Freeman told investigators that the fight became physical, and Tibbs strangled Rison until she was dead. Freeman then helped Tibbs to dispose of her body.

Current Status:
Twenty-one years after her death, on November 7, 2014, Jason Tibbs was convicted of murdering Rayna Rison. He choked her to death because she refused to be his girlfriend.

On December 12, Tibbs was sentenced to forty years in prison. Because of Indiana's sentencing guidelines, he will receive a day of freedom for each day served, and so will ultimately be in prison for just less than twenty years.

In return for his testimony against Tibbs, Eric Freeman received full immunity and was not charged.

The Power of Touch DNA

Victim: Krystal Lynn Beslanowitch
Location: Salt Lake City, Utah
Suspect: Joseph Michael Simpson
Date of Crime: December 1995
Date of Identification: 2013

Backstory:
Krystal Lynn Beslanowitch was born in Spokane, Washington on June 5, 1978 and was 17 years old in 1995. Her mother, Linde Toreson, has told newspapers that by age 15, Beslanowitch was already involved in drugs and prostitution. She had recently moved to Salt Lake City with her boyfriend, from her hometown of Spokane, Washington.

Despite her lifestyle, whenever she saw her, Beslanowitch's mother always welcomed her with open arms. Her mother reports that she was always happy, and Beslanowitch thought that being able to live as she did was more important than having a 'normal' life.

On The Day In Question:
One day Beslanowitch failed to return home after a late night trip to a convenience store. It took a further two days for her boyfriend to report her missing.

Then, on the early morning of December 6, 1995, her naked body was found along the Provo River. She had been bludgeoned, and her body was broken and bloody. She was lying face down over the rocks.

Investigation:
Despite an investigation that covered the whole state and ran for two years, no significant leads or suspects were ever uncovered.

The case went cold, but for one investigator the murder of Beslanowitch had become personal. County Sheriff Todd Bonner couldn't let the case go. He has since told the Associated Press that her story haunted him, and he kept investigating himself.

Without his efforts, it's possible the case may never have been solved. As a deputy, Bonner had been one of the first investigators to arrive on the scene the day Beslanowitch's body was discovered. In 2009 he was elected as Wasatch County Sheriff, but he never forgot her case and regularly checked in on any progress.

In 2006, Beslanowitch's case was reopened. New DNA technology meant that cold cases were now generating new leads. In 2008, two full time detectives were assigned to the case. Technology had improved again, and more DNA was extracted from crime scene evidence in the Beslanowitch murder. Despite the efforts of Bonner and others however, no significant progress was made.

In 2013 a forensics lab was able to extract what's called "touch DNA" from granite rocks used to crush Beslanowitch's skull. This is DNA left behind from when someone simply touches an object at the crime scene. The DNA was run against databases and a match came back.

It matched a man named Joseph Michael Simpson, who had previously been convicted of an unrelated murder and was on parole just months before Beslanowitch's murder. In 2013 he was forty-six, unemployed, and living with his mother in Sarasota, Florida.

Until DNA identified him, Simpson had not even been on investigator's radar. The technology used to identify his DNA profile had not existed at the time of Beslanowitch's murder. It was collected using a forensic vacuum, and took a full day to collect the sample.

Originally invented to remove bacteria from food, the inventor's son shared the invention with a friend who worked for the FBI. When they tested it, they discovered that it could recover 40% more DNA from a saliva stain on a shirt than the traditional swab method. It could also retrieve 88% more DNA from a blood stain on fabric. The vacuum recovered Simpson's full DNA profile from a rock he touched at the crime scene.

Despite the match, prosecutors insisted that investigators retrieve a fresh sample. Bonner and another detective then flew to Sarasota and followed Simpson around for multiple days, before they were able to recover a DNA sample from a discarded cigarette. They ran it and the DNA was a match. Simpson was arrested for Beslanowitch's murder. Todd Bonner was the one to handcuff him and place him under arrest.

Current Status:
Prosecutors announced in April of 2014 that they would not be seeking the death penalty in the trial. At the time of writing, Simpson is being held without bail.

The Creep One Block Away

Victim: Anna Palmer
Location: Salt Lake City, Utah
Suspect: Matthew Breck
Date of Crime: September 10, 1998
Date of Conviction: August 2001

Backstory:
Anna Palmer was born on August 8, 1988 to parents Nancy and David Palmer. Her family consisted of brothers Mike and Matthew and sisters Christine and Rachel. Anna was in the fifth grade at Whittier Elementary School in Salt Lake City, Utah.

Ten-year-old Anna was a friendly child. Her mother has described her as a "little socialite", often playing with all the other children in the neighborhood.

On The Day In Question:
On September 10, 1998, Palmer phoned her mother around 5:00pm and asked her if she was allowed to go and play with some friends. That was the last time her mother would hear her voice. At 7:00pm her mother returned home and found Palmer's dead body lying on the porch of their home.

Her body was already cold to the touch, and her mother has reported that her face was a 'waxy, pale, yellowy color', as though Palmer's blood was no longer flowing. She immediately called 911.

She was advised by the operator to start CPR, and although paramedics arrived within minutes, Palmer was pronounced dead when they arrived on the scene.

Investigation:
At first investigators wondered if the injuries could be dog bites. However, an autopsy revealed that Palmer had been

stabbed to death on the front porch of her home. She had fought back against her attacker, and been stabbed in the throat five times, and also beaten severely. One of the stab wounds had severed her spinal cord and killed her.

A police search began, and neighbors remember hearing helicopters and seeing searchlights for most of the night.

Despite the murder happening in broad daylight in public and near a busy intersection, witnesses were scarce. The crime scene had little evidence, and what did exist was not much use with the science techniques of the day. Nevertheless, swabs were still taken from Palmer's body and clothing, and her fingernails were clipped. DNA profiling was not as advanced in 1998 as it is now.

Despite police investigations, no suspects were revealed and the case went cold.

An offered reward of $11,000 turned up some leads, but nothing they uncovered led to an arrest in the case.

Then, in 2009, detectives had the samples analyzed again. Using a new technique, forensic scientists were able to extract DNA that did not belong to Palmer from the swabs and fingernail clippings. Palmer's attempt to fight back had trapped her attacker's skin under her nails.

When the DNA was tested, there was a match. It belonged to a man named Matthew Breck. Breck was already serving a ten-year sentence in Idaho for child sex-related crimes. In 1998, he had been nineteen years old and living only one block from Palmer's house.

Two witnesses, who were children at the time of the crime, testified that they had seen a teenager walking near Palmer's house that day when she had been heading home. A taped police interview with a then ten-year-old friend of Palmer's said they had played together on swings in her backyard, and then when it was near 7:00pm, they hugged and went their separate ways on a street corner.

She told police that at that time she'd noticed a man behind them who looked liked he might want to grab them. Palmer let the man pass her, and then yelled at her friend to run home. When her friend looked back, Palmer was on her way home and the man was gone.

Several other witnesses who were children at the time also came forward to report a man that had "creeped" them out. Multiple witnesses reported him as wearing a baseball jersey and having dark stringy hair. Breck was known to regularly wear baseball jerseys.

Current Status:
In August of 2001, Breck pled guilty to aggravated murder. The rest of his life will be spent in prison.

Had the evidence not been found in Palmer's case, he would have already served the time of his other jail term and would have been again living in society.

A Suicide Unproven

Victim: Pamela J. Shelly
Location: DeWitt County, Texas
Suspect: Ronnie Hendrick
Date of Crime: January 6, 2001
Date of Guilty Plea: September 10, 2013

Backstory:
Pamela Jean Shelly was born on July 25, 1969 in Harris County Texas as Pamela Jean Curlee. Her parents were Pearly Jean Surber and Carl Edward Curlee.

In 2001 she was living with her boyfriend, Ronnie Hendrick, and her two children, Kayla (12) and Dustin (9). They lived in a rural area of DeWitt County, Texas.

Hendrick's family lived just a mile away, and Shelly's own family lived eight hundred miles away in Arkansas. Shelly had only lived in Texas for five months.

On The Day In Question:
On January 6, 2001, Pamela Shelly died in the bathroom of her home. The cause of death was a single gunshot wound to the head. Hendrick's stepfather called it in as an attempted suicide, and Shelly was still breathing when she was loaded into an ambulance.

Being a rural area and 'in the middle of nowhere', Hendrick volunteered to accompany the ambulance to direct the driver. That meant when the sheriff's deputies arrived, he was not there to answer any questions, or to be tested for gunshot residue.

When asked, emergency responders who attended the scene did not have any reason to doubt that the gunshot wound had been self-inflicted. The scene didn't "feel like" a shooting of unknown origin, everyone was relatively calm and there was very little panic.

Apparently the family never considered that this was anything other than self-inflicted. No one was afraid an unknown shooter might be lurking. It was because Shelly's shooter was very much known and standing right next to them.

Investigation:
From the beginning, had some evidence been handled differently it may have changed the course of the investigation. Investigators at the scene interviewed the adults present, who were all direct relatives of Hendricks.

They did not however talk to Shelly's children at all, a move that has since been criticized. At twelve and nine years old, they were certainly old enough to be able to express to investigators what they'd witnessed.

Hendrick's family all told officers that Shelly had been unhappy and suicidal for some time. They also said that her family had a history of suicide and her sister had also killed herself. It would later be revealed that all of this was untrue.

Hendrick's family also claimed that Shelly's oldest daughter was a "difficult child" and was forcing Shelly to return to Arkansas, prompting the suicide.

Shelly was life-flighted to San Antonio, but she died on arrival. An autopsy was performed, but the medical examiner was told upfront that it was a suspected suicide. Did that color his findings? When the contact wound and path of the bullet reflected a typical suicide, Shelly's death was ruled as such.

Officers asked Hendrick to take a polygraph test, and he agreed, but then failed to show up to at least two separate appointments. Soon after this, he disappeared.

With no local friends or family to make sure Shelly's side of the story was heard, the case languished. It would be another seven years before anyone took a more detailed look at the case.

In 2008, a law enforcement officer named Carl Bowen became an investigator under the DeWitt County Sheriff. Bowen had been on the force when Shelly's death occurred, and although he hadn't been assigned to the case he had known about it.

He'd taken an interest in the investigation, and it had always bothered him that Hendrick had never taken the polygraph test.

Even more suspicious was the fact he'd disappeared soon after Shelly's death. All these years the case had left questions in his mind, and now with his new appointment he was able to do something about it. He approached the Sheriff, Jode Zavesky, about re-opening the case, and was given permission.

Then, in the summer of 2008, Hendrick appeared in the DeWitt County Jail. He'd been arrested and charged with domestic abuse, beating up his new live-in girlfriend. Bowen also discovered at this time that during the time between Shelly's death and his recent appearance, Hendrick had been in jail in South Dakota for a felony DWI. Now he knew that Hendrick was a convicted alcohol abuser and violent man. Alarm bells were now ringing.

Bowen approached Hendrick about finally undergoing the polygraph, and Hendrick agreed. Perhaps predictably the results indicated deception from Hendrick for the events surrounding Shelly's death. When questioned after these results, he asserted his right to counsel.

However, after the polygraph Hendrick told three different people that he'd lied to the police. He was still denying he'd killed her, but now said that he had been in the room with her, a significant change in his story. Previously, he'd told police that he had been outside when she had shot herself.

Bowen took the case to the district attorney's office, but he was rejected. They did not feel there was enough evidence to make the case. Although they believed that Hendrick had at least been involved in her death, the autopsy report still stated the death as suicide, and that was a major sticking point.

Then in 2012, Bowen approached their office again to ask for their support in contacting a cold case TV show regarding Shelly's case. The assistant district attorney (ADA) in charge of the case didn't thinking anything would come of it, but saw no reason to deny the request. He wanted to be able to say that every stone had been unturned in the hunt for the truth.

Despite the district attorney's skepticism of the show ever making it to air, the producers of the show jumped right in. The idea behind the show was that a former ADA, Kelly Siegler, and former crime scene investigator, Yolanda McClary, would come in and help small and often under-staffed law enforcement agencies take a fresh look at a cold case.

They soon learned that Siegler's reputation was well earned. She interviewed witnesses, and reinvestigated the crime scene and all facets of the case. They also gave the investigators access to the latest technical advances in forensic investigations with a quick turnaround. The gun was analyzed for touch DNA, the slug for ballistics, and a bloody t-shirt found in the laundry hamper for DNA. They also did computer modeling of the scene.

Despite all this, there was still not a break in the case. The touch DNA test found nothing, and the DNA on the shirt was all Shelly's. The slug matched the revolver found at the scene, and the computer modeling revealed nothing significant.

The TV team investigated the evidence given by the Hendrick's family, and discovered their lies. There had been no history of depression in Shelly's family, and she had never been on anti-depressant medication herself. They also found no evidence of previous suicides in her family. The case for Shelly's death truly being a suicide was starting to look shaky.

From there, Seigler's team started to look at the likelihood that it was murder. They found that Hendrick had committed several serious assaults on other women, both before and after Shelly's death. In one that was eerily similar to the circumstances of Shelly's death, he nearly killed the woman.

Johnny Bonds, a former interviewer with the Houston Police Department with an excellent reputation, re-interviewed multiple people involved in the original incident, including Hendrick himself.

So had someone else been involved in Shelly's death? Had she been murdered and the original investigation missed it? Still the biggest weakness in the case was the gunshot wound.

It's very difficult to get the gun barrel right up against the temple of an unwilling victim. Even if they are held still, most still manage to pull their head back slightly. How then did Shelly have a contact wound if she had not pulled the trigger herself? There was really only one way.

If Hendrick had crept up on Shelly while she was in the bathroom using the mirror, and she had seen him and turned to face him just before the gun went off, that would produce the same wound pattern. Despite now having an explanation for the wound pattern besides suicide, the DA was still not ready to take the case to trial.

Then, a few weeks after the filming the show, the final piece fell into place. Bowen found Shelly's ex-husband, Jessie. He was incarcerated in a prison in Texas. He told Bowen that he had spoken to Shelly on the day of her death. According to his testimony, he and Shelly were getting back together. He was the father of her eldest child, and she was planning to move back home with the kids and be a family together again.

During the phone call, Hendrick had grabbed the phone and told Jessie that the only way Shelly would be returning to Arkansas was if she was in a pine box. Jessie was also polygraphed, and when he passed with flying colors, the district attorney was ready. The case for Shelly's murder was taken to a grand jury.

Hendrick was indicted by the grand jury in November of 2012. He was incarcerated until his trial in September 2013.

Meanwhile, the reality TV show episode was due to run just days before jury selection. With the gathering media attention, the DA started to worry that ironically the whole case would fail because of the attention given to it by the very thing that helped to break it open in the first place. The producers of the show however refused to delay the broadcast, and it went to air only days before the real trial began.

Thankfully, on the day of the trial the judge asked the jury members to raise their hands if they had watched the show. A third of them did so. As they were interviewed and most admitted that they already thought Hendrick had killed Shelly, a mistrial was declared.

The only solution that the DA could see was to change venues. However, the show had been broadcast nation-wide. The judge reset the case to be tried again in June of 2014, hoping that the fanfare would have died down by then.

The DA then approached Hendrick's attorney. He told them that when he brought the case to trial the delay would mean he'd only have more evidence, and also pointed out that nearly everyone who had seen the TV show already thought Hendrick was guilty.

In the end, Hendrick pled guilty to murder just a day later. He was sentenced to twenty-two years in jail.

Current Status:
A timeline established twelve years after the murder showed that over an hour passed between the shooting and when emergency responders were called. Did that gap give the family time to get their stories straight and rearrange any crucial evidence?

The DA that prosecuted the case has the utmost respect for the professionals involved in the show. However, he believes that the producers were wrong in not delaying the broadcast. Had it been delayed just two weeks, he believes he could have impaneled an impartial jury. Had Hendrick been found guilty in a trial rather than taking a plea bargain, he would likely have received life in prison.

Many think that were it not for the actions of Carl Bowen and Sheriff Jode Zavesky in taking a personal interest and re-opening the case, justice would never have happened for Shelly. There was no political pressure or public speculation driving the case. As far as the general population was concerned, Shelly had committed suicide. The only thing on her side was one investigator with a nagging feeling that something just wasn't right.

Solved But Unexplained

Victim: Sara Lynn Wineski
Location: St. Petersburg, Florida
Suspect: Raymond Samuels
Date of Crime: May 22nd, 2005
Date Identified: 2013

Backstory:
Sara Lynn Wineski was born in San Diego, California on June 25th, 1955 to parents Walter Wineski and Katherine McManus. Records indicate she married Edward J. Murphy on July 12th, 1975 when she was 20 years old.

The couple had two children, daughter Candace M. born May 9th, 1976 and son Edward James born March 21st, 1978. The marriage was not to last and they divorced on April 12th, 1984.

It's not known what occurred in the intervening years but in 2005 Sara Lynn Wineski had born two more children and then become a homeless woman living in St. Petersburg, Florida. She had moved there from Sarasota less than two weeks before her death. She was forty-nine years old.

On The Day In Question:
On Sunday May 22nd, 2005, Wineski's body was found in a secluded area, under a wooden deck belonging to a Ronald McDonald House. She had been dead for less than a day when she was found.

Investigation:
Investigations revealed that Wineski had been raped and then strangled. She had been killed brutally, her body suffering significant trauma, particularly her upper body.

A guest of the Ronald McDonald House recalled hearing screams around 11:00pm the night before. The deck where her body was found overlooked Roser Park, a common sleeping place for homeless people.

At the time of the attack, police suspected the case was linked to an earlier violent sexual assault that had occurred near Campbell Park on May 7th. Campbell Park was close to the scene of Wineski's murder, and police said both crimes had "disturbing similarities" that they were not releasing.

The victim of that attack (a resident, rather than homeless as Wineski had been) had survived the attack, and described the perpetrator as a black man with a dark complexion, twenty-six to thirty years old, around 5' 7" tall, and with a thin build. Investigators were worried that a serial rapist was on the loose.

Police handed out flyers at parks and shelters around the crime area, looking for people who might have seen Wineski shortly before she was killed.

DNA evidence was collected at the scene of Wineski's murder, but there was no progress on identifying a suspect.

Then, in 2013, there was a sudden break in the case. The DNA from the case found a match, a man named Raymond Samuels. In 2005, he had been visiting St. Petersburg. He had then been in prison in Ohio since 2006, charged with attempted murder and kidnapping, where his DNA was recorded in the system.

Samuels, who would have been twenty-three at the time of the attack, was also a transient person with no fixed address, and had been in the area for less than two months before Wineski's murder.

Current Status:

Wineski was survived by four children, and now also has four grandchildren. Her family is glad that her killer has been found, saying that her life was not a waste, and not something anyone had the right to take from her, despite how she was living when she ran into Samuels on that fateful night.

Samuels is currently awaiting trial at Pinellas County Jail in Clearwater, Florida.

A Fateful Walk

Victims: Skyla Whitaker, Taylor Paschal-Placker
Location: Weleetka, Oklahoma
Suspect: Kevin Sweat
Date of Crime: June 8, 2008
Date of Conviction: October 17, 2014

Backstory:
Skyla Jade Whitaker was born in Joplin Missouri on April 5, 1997. Her parents, William and Rose Whitaker also had daughters Rosita, Christina and Jayme and son Edward. Skyla was in the 5th grade at Graham School.

Taylor Dawn Paschal-Placker was born March 6, 1995 in Oklahoma City, Oklahoma. Her parents were Vicky and Peter Placker. She also attended Graham School and was in the 6th grade.

Both girls were active in 4H, cheerleading and SWAT (Students Working Against Tobacco) and were best friends. Skyla wanted to be a veterinarian some day.

On The Day In Question:
On Sunday, June 8, 2008, the girls were walking together down a rural dirt track. Despite its condition, the road was well used by locals, and the girls had taken the route together many times before. They had had a sleep over together at Paschal-Placker's house the night before, and were on their way to a riverbank where they wanted to collect pebbles and shells.

Then, that afternoon a disturbing call came into 911 at the Okfuskee County Sheriff's Department. A woman on the other end of the call was screaming, "Somebody's killed two girls!" That woman was Paschal-Placker's grandmother, who had found the bodies of the two girls lying in a ditch along a rural road. Their bodies were riddled with bullets, the girls together had been shot a total of thirteen times.

Investigation:
Police determined that more than one gun was used to kill the girls, one of which was a .40 caliber Glock semi-automatic handgun. They did not release any information regarding the second gun, but did state that both victims had been shot with both guns. Were they looking at two perpetrators or a single attacker with multiple weapons?

Police and the community both struggled to understand why someone would kill the two young girls. Neither of them was a member of any gangs or lived "high risk" lifestyles. They were both popular and well liked by both their peers and their teachers. Whitaker wanted to be a vet when she grew up. Paschal-Placker, described by her friends as "the smartest girl in school", wanted to be a forensic scientist.

Evidence found at the scene included tire tracks, shoe prints, as well as shell casings and bullets. A witness also reported a Native American person seen in the area at the time of the shooting, and a police released a composite sketch. Due to the remoteness of the location, investigators believed that the perpetrator had to be a local. They interviewed every known violent felon in the area, but came up empty.

With no leads or suspects, the case went cold.

Years passed, and then a break came from a very unexpected place. In 2011, Kevin Sweat, who lived in the nearby town of Okmulgee, was unhappy in his relationship. He was engaged to Ashley Taylor, but things hadn't always been smooth sailing. In fact, Sweat had written on his blog a year earlier that the engagement was "the biggest mistake of his life". People described Sweat as secretive and unpredictable, and he would often write cryptic messages.

During the summer of 2011, Sweat told his friends that he and Taylor were eloping to New Orleans. They left town together, but Sweat returned alone. He told friends that along the way they had started arguing, and Taylor had left the car and walked away. Suspicious of his claims, Taylor's family reported her missing.

When police visited Sweat to investigate their claims, they found a man who was obsessed with guns and knives. During questioning, Sweat admitted that he had killed Taylor by slitting her throat, and had then pushed her into a lake. However, when they searched his father's property, police found a burnt-out bonfire that contained human remains. Also found in the fire were the remains of a pair of glasses. The prescription matched Taylor's.

It was while making sure they'd thoroughly investigated the scene of Taylor's murder that the police uncovered perhaps the most surprising part of the whole investigation. In the backyard where Taylor's remains had been found, police uncovered shell casings. When the casings were analyzed, the police couldn't believe it – they matched the ones recovered from the murders of Whitaker and Paschal-Placker three years earlier.

Could the man who killed his fiancé also be involved in the murder of two young girls?

Once Sweat was informed of the match, he began talking to police as easily as he had about Taylor's murder. However, his tale was a strange one. He said that he had been driving down the road that afternoon when he had seen two monsters. When the monsters started moving towards him, he panicked and grabbed a gun and fired at them. He then grabbed another gun from his glove box and fired that as well.

Was a mental illness or hallucination the reason two innocent girls had been killed so brutally, and why so many bullets had been fired? For both girls, multiple shots could have been the cause of death. Sweat was adamant that he had never seen two girls on the dirt road that afternoon, only monsters.

Current Status:
In 2014, Sweat pleaded guilty to three counts of first-degree murder. In return for waiving his right to a jury trial, the prosecution did not seek the death penalty. Instead, a judge would decide the verdict and sentencing.

Court documents suggest that Sweat may have held a grudge for unknown reasons against Paschal-Placker's family. However, because of his guilty plea, this information was not made public. The only known motive for murdering Taylor was that he didn't want to marry her.

Was that all it was, or had she discovered that he'd killed the two girls years before? Did he want her out of the way, or perhaps Sweat simply had an unpredictable violent streak that erupted twice with deadly consequences?

In October of 2014, Sweat attacked one of his lawyers while meeting in the judge's chambers. He cut the man across the neck with a razor blade. The man survived, but after the incident no longer represented Sweat.

Sweat then tried to withdraw his guilty plea, but it was rejected. The judge sentenced Sweat, who was then twenty-eight, to three life sentences without the possibility of parole.

A memorial to Whitaker and Paschal-Placker remains on the side of the road where they were tragically killed. An angel statue stands surrounded by flowers, toys, and a music box.

Thankfully, the Whitaker and Paschal-Placker families did not have to wait decades for justice for their daughters.

Led Astray

Victim: Jessica Lyn Keen
Location: Columbus, Ohio
Suspect: Marvin Lee Smith, Jr.
Date of Crime: March 17, 1991
Date of Conviction: February 7th, 2009

Backstory:
Jessica Lyn Keen was a fifteen-year-old girl from Columbus, Ohio. She was a model student, on the honor roll and also a cheerleader.

When she met Shawn Thompson, an eighteen-year-old young man from central Ohio, her life seemed to change. After she starting seeing Thompson, she quit cheerleading and her grades dropped. She reportedly skipped school frequently to see him.

Her parents objected to her relationship with Thompson, and in March 1991 they placed her in a home for troubled teens. Called Huckleberry House, it was a safe house and crisis center for runaways and troubled teens in Columbus, Ohio.

On The Day In Question:
On March 15, 1991 Keen left Huckleberry House after having a fight with her boyfriend. She had said she was going to the mall. She never returned, and the last time anyone had seen her alive was at a bus stop.

On March 17, Keen's body was found at the back of Foster Chapel Cemetery. The cemetery was located twenty miles away from Huckleberry House.

Her body had been badly beaten, and she had been raped. She was dressed only in a single sock and a torn, dirty bra. Although she still had on her ring and watch, a pendant had been taken.

Investigation:
Police were immediately suspicious of her boyfriend, Thompson. However, DNA evidence cleared him of any involvement.

Evidence at the crime scene suggested that she had run from her attacker and tried to hide in the cemetery. Her other sock was found elsewhere on the grounds, and the imprint of knees in the mud behind a gravestone were also found nearby. Her body lay near a fence, where presumably her attacker had caught up with her.

With no further suspects to test the DNA evidence against, and not much other evidence to go on, the case grew cold. It would stay that way for over a decade.

Meanwhile, Marvin Lee Smith, Jr. was serving a nine-year sentence for two unrelated attempted assaults, both against women and in the Columbus area. During his prison term, a law was passed and went into effect that required inmates to submit their DNA to a statewide database.

As technology improved, in 2008 the DNA from Keen's case was run, and it matched the sample from Smith. By that time, Smith had been released from prison, and was living in Burlington, North Carolina. North Carolina police arrested him and charged him with unlawful sexual conduct with Keen, taking another fresh DNA sample to verify the match.

With the DNA match verified, an extradition hearing was set for April 30, 2008. Smith appeared in court in Madison County and admitted that he had raped and murdered Keen.

He told the court that he had abducted her from the bus stop in his car. Keen escaped from his car and ran into the cemetery, where she collided with a fence poll and fell over. He beat Keen to death with a gravestone, later discarding it over a fence.

Current Status:
By confessing, Smith avoided the death penalty. He pled guilty to one count of aggravated murder, with specifications of rape. He was sentenced to thirty years to life in prison.

When he was arrested, Keen's sister was quoted as saying "Everything in my life is measured against her loss. Time is marked before and after her death."

The Body in the Side Table

Victim: Cynthia Epps
Location: Buffalo, New York
Suspect: James Fountain
Date of Crime: June 30, 1994
Date Convicted: July 13, 2012

Backstory:
Cynthia Epps was a twenty-nine year old woman who lived in Buffalo, New York. She was born on August 21, 1964 and had two young daughters. She lived at 25 Colfax Street in Buffalo, which is 1.7 miles from 142 Montana Street where her body was found.

On The Day In Question:
On June 30, 1994, a man named James Fountain called police to report a grisly find in his yard. A woman's badly injured body had been stuffed into a side table next to his garage. Her body was wrapped in a blanket, and when police investigated, they were horrified to find she had been nearly hacked up. Epps had been stabbed many times, and had nearly been decapitated.

Investigation:
An autopsy was done and DNA evidence was collected. Fountain denied ever meeting Epps prior to finding her body, and cooperated with the investigation. He was not charged and neither was anyone else. The case grew cold.

In 2010, Epps's case was reopened. The two detectives handling the case were Charles Aronica and Lissa Redmond, both of the Buffalo Police Department Cold Case Squad. They worked in conjunction with prosecutor Gary Hackbush. Fountain was looked at again, and this time the investigators made a concerning discovery.

Back in 1977, Fountain had been convicted in Queens County for manslaughter in the second degree. He also had a conviction from 1984 for rape in the first degree, and attempted rape in the first degree in 1996. Clearly, he was a dangerous and violent man.

Fountain was currently living at the Central New York Psychiatric Center in Marcy, New York, having been placed there on an indefinite civil confinement. State law required that he submit a DNA sample, so his DNA was now available in the state database. Investigators ran it against the vaginal swab taken at Epps's autopsy, and it matched. Fountain had been no innocent bystander.

Based on the DNA evidence discovery, Fountain was re-questioned by investigators. He still denied ever knowing Epps, and also denied having any contact with her at all before he found her body.

However when he was told of the DNA match he finally gave in, and admitted to having sex with Epps and then brutally stabbing her. He told investigators that he tried to sever her head and leg to make the body easier to get rid of.

James Fountain appeared before a grand jury, and an indictment of murder in the second degree was returned. He pled guilty and on July 13, 2012, he was sentenced to life in prison.

Current Status:
Epps's sister stated in court that she forgave her sister's murderer, and did not harbor any ill will towards him.
Fountain's convictions for manslaughter and rape both occurred before Epps's murder. You have to wonder why police did not discover his prior convictions and take a closer look at him when her body was discovered. Instead, her murder remained unsolved for eighteen years.

Young Mom Home Alone

Victim: Amy Weidner
Location: Indianapolis, Indiana
Suspect: Troy Jackson, Rodney Denk
Date of Crime: November 13, 1989
Date of Conviction: June 14, 2013

Backstory:

Amy Weidner was a sixteen-year-old who lived with her family in Indianapolis, Indiana. Her mother Gloria was raising her and her siblings on her own.

Weidner had three siblings, two sisters and a brother. Her family remembers her as a girl who loved school, who would probably one day be a teacher herself. She helped out around the home, and was much loved by her mother and siblings.

Becoming pregnant at just fourteen years old, Weidner was the proud mother of a two-year-old daughter, named Emily. The father was seventeen years old and a good friend of her older brothers.

Her mother did not want her to stay involved with him, wanting Weidner to concentrate on finishing her education. Emily was born in October 1987, and Weidner returned to school just six days later.

After her daughter was born, family and teachers say that Weidner became more focused and responsible. She still found time to have fun with her friends, her mother helping her out with babysitting.

On The Day In Question:

On November 13, 1989, Weidner woke up feeling unwell. Her mother offered to take Emily to a babysitter for the day, but Weidner said she would keep her at home with her. Leaving for the day, Gloria called the house around 9:30am to check up on Weidner, but there was no answer.

After she didn't answer a second call, Gloria rang a neighbor and asked her to go and check on Weidner and Emily. The neighbor went around and knocked on the door, but no one answered. She called Gloria back and told her.

Gloria immediately left work and came home, only to discover a horrific scene. Weidner was lying dead on her bed. She had been both beaten and then strangled. Her daughter Emily was still in the house and unharmed.

Gloria removed Emily from the house and called 911.

Investigation:
The news of Weidner's death spread quickly, and by the time school was done for the day a reporter was at the school asking questions. Perhaps because Weidner was a teenage mother and must have led a stressful life, the first thought of some at the school was that she had committed suicide. It was soon confirmed however that Weidner had been murdered.

Captain Jack Geilker from the Sheriff's office, one of the first on the scene, said it was one that he won't forget. Weidner had lacerations to her head, and was lying naked. There were bloody prints across the crime scene, and it was obvious her death had been a violent one. Police discovered that she had also been raped before death. Worse yet, two-year-old Emily had been left on her own with her mother's dead body.

A police officer specializing in interviewing victims was at the scene, and he talked to Emily. He used finger puppets to help Emily explain what she remembered, the two year old showing how she ran back and forth from her own room to Weidner's, and then to her grandmother's bedroom. Emily said that "Mamy was mean", her word for fighting.

Investigators' first thoughts were that Weidner's death was a robbery gone wrong. Stereo equipment and money were both missing from the home, and a back door was found open.

Police questioned many people close to Weidner, including her friends and family. Some of the interviews were accusatory, including the one with her older brother, but no one was arrested or charged with Weidner's death.

The outpouring of grief over Weidner's death was large, with many students at the school finding it hard to understand. Attempting to find further leads, detectives attended her funeral. One of the people who came to their attention was Tony Abercrombie, Emily's father. However, he spoke fondly of Weidner and had an alibi. He had been at work when a friend called him to tell him what had happened.

Attention then turned to another man, Troy Jackson. Jackson lived in the house behind the Weidners, and police discovered that he had known about the stolen stereo equipment already on the day of the murder.

Police photographed his hands, noting that he didn't have any injuries himself indicative of being involved in a struggle. He also passed a polygraph test. DNA was still in its infancy, but a hair sample he submitted did not match anything found in Weidner's room. Investigators moved on.

Weeks turned into months and with no arrest. Weidner's friends and family found themselves wondering if there would forever be an unknown killer in their midst. Police believed that Weidner had known her killer, and with no leads, fear and suspicion grew every day.

In 2002, a call came in to the Indianapolis Police cold case squad. The officer who took the call, Lieutenant Spurgeon, was not personally familiar with Weidner's case, but the caller seemed to know many details. However, there was not much revealed that couldn't have been seen in the media of the time.

The call ended up being a dead end, but it sparked Spurgeon's interest in the case. He read up on the case and investigated a few persons of interest, but nothing new was uncovered. Spurgeon moved on to another area, but the case remained with the cold case unit.

In 2011, in response to a newspaper article, friends of Weidner created a "Remembering Amy Weidner" page on Facebook. No one in the cold case department was overly familiar with Facebook, but they knew someone who understood it intimately, Detective William Carter, who was a nuisance abatement officer. He was asked to go over the memorial page on Facebook, but not knowing anything about the case himself he decided to read the case file as well.

Carter found he could not forget Weidner's face from her photo, and started working on the case on his own time, re-examining more than two decades worth of evidence. Collating all the old evidence into digital form, he noticed that some original possibilities had been overlooked.

For example, many friends of Weidner's had been talked to, but none had ever given a DNA sample. Weidner had already been involved with one of her brother's friends, could she have been in a secret relationship with another? For Officer Carter, the case became personal. He was determined to solve it.

He re-contacted Weidner's family and friends to see if they had since remembered anything else, and also started collecting DNA from anyone who police had originally investigated. During the original investigation, police had canvassed the neighborhood and recorded the names of everyone who lived there. Carter found that for the most part, people had moved on. So, he started the long process of tracking them down.

One person who Carter found was Joy Haney, who had been a friend of Weidner's and lived across the street. He asked her if anyone now stuck out in her mind from that date. Most of the names she gave him, he already knew. But one had never been mentioned before. The name was Rodney Denk.

Also a friend of her older brother's, the family recalled him as being a regular kid. He hung out with Weidner's brother often, going fishing and riding their bikes around. The family described Denk as being a quiet young man, mostly keeping to himself.

Carter investigated and found him living with his mother. He worked at an auto shop, and was divorced with a son. Carter left his card, and when Denk called him, Carter told him that he wanted to speak to him regarding Weidner. Denk agreed to meet at his house, but when Carter arrived he was nowhere to be seen.

Suspicions raised, Carter ran Denk's background and found that he had been arrested previously two times, for battery in 1991 and larceny in 1997. Now with interests piqued, he ran the prints from Denk's arrest against a bloody handprint from Weidner's wall. Still, he was stunned when it came back as a match. Finally after more than twenty years, they had a suspect.

Likely deciding that the past had finally caught up with him, Denk had disappeared. Using a fugitive task force unit, Carter tracked him with his credit card. Denk had used his card to hire a car that happened to have a tracking device installed.

Using that, police found him visiting a friend in Indianapolis. When police approached him, Denk pulled out a knife. Yelling that he didn't do it, Denk attempted to cut his wrist, but was apprehended by police before he could do any serious damage to himself or others.

Denk was taken to the hospital, and Weidner's family and friends were stunned when they learned who the police had arrested. Denk had been a good friend to them, and had even attended Weidner's funeral, signing the guestbook.

Looking through the old notes, Carter made a discovery. Denk had been named as a person of interest to the police before, back when Weidner was originally killed. Despite that, he was never interviewed or investigated, and was not mentioned anywhere else in the case notes. The person who had mentioned him? Tony Abercombie, Emily's father.

A DNA sample was taken from Denk, and it matched semen taking from Weidner's sheets back in 1989. He pleaded guilty to Weidner's murder, and was sentenced to sixty-five years in prison.

Current Status:
Rodney Denk was just seventeen when he murdered Amy Weidner. It turned out that it had been a robbery gone wrong, as police had suspected from the very beginning. However, no one had suspected that the murderer would be a close family friend. After being interviewed by police, Denk admitted to raping and then killing Weidner when she discovered him trying to steal radios from her brother's room.

Perhaps chillingly, it was discovered during the investigation into Weidner's murder that Denk's own son, Dillon Denk, had been charged with murdering his own mother by beating her to death. Dillon was sixteen years old at the time of the crime just one year younger than his father was when he killed Weidner.

Weidner's family was profoundly affected by her death. For a long time her other children refused to come home from school before Gloria was home from work. Unable to afford to move, they continued to live in the house where the murder took place.

Gloria legally adopted Emily. The child who had been her granddaughter became her own daughter, and she became a sister rather than niece to Weidner's siblings. The now grown Emily refers to Gloria as her mom and her aunts and uncle as her brother and sisters.

The family made sure Emily knew her mother growing up, keeping her memory alive with stories. Emily herself has no memories of her mother.

Emily has noticed a difference in the family since Weidner's death. Watching family home movies, she could see a time where everyone was happy at her first and second birthday parties, and after that they didn't seem as happy again.

Detective Carter was offered a position on the homicide squad, but he chose to remain in his current position. On his own time, he is now investigating other cold cases in Indianapolis.

The Truth Hidden For 25 Years

Victim: Martha Jean Lambert
Location: Elkton, Florida
Suspect: David Lambert
Date of Crime: November 27, 1985
Date Identified: 2010

Backstory:

Martha Jean Lambert was twelve years old, and lived in Elkton, Florida. She'd grown up with a difficult home life. Both she and her two older brothers had previously suffered child abuse and been placed in foster care. One of her brothers had also run away from home in the past, and both brothers had previous brushes with the law.

Lambert was in seventh grade at her junior high school. She was blonde and 4'5" tall. Her brother David Lambert has said that despite her small size, she was extremely feisty. Other extended family members however recall her as shy. She was good at school, and always wore a smile, according to their recollections.

Her neighbors said that she was a girl who was friendly, but was always dirty. They recalled screaming and abuse at home, and thought her family was "odd". There was a large age gap between her father, who was seventy-four, and her mother, who was just thirty-three. Her father was an alcoholic, and her neighbors also thought her brothers were "a bit strange". They were however fond of Lambert herself, despite their thoughts about her family.

On The Day In Question:

On November 27, 1985, Lambert was having dinner with her brother, according to his report to investigators. After they'd eaten, she told him she was going out, but refused to disclose her destination.

A witness reported seeing her walking west along a road named Kerri-Lynn Road in St. Augustine, Florida. She was wearing a two-piece bathing suit. The temperature that day was average for the time of year, neither too hot nor too cold.

That would be the last time anyone saw Lambert alive.

Investigation:
As the last family member to see her alive, her brother David Lambert (then fourteen), was questioned extensively by police, but he was never arrested or charged with anything having to do with her disappearance. Thanksgiving was the next day, and he told police that Lambert had wanted to get out of the house to escape her father. He had been yelling over their burned turkey.

Her mother was insistent that Lambert would not have run away, or gotten into a friend's car without permission. Friends and police searched the area and backwoods for days, but nothing was ever found.

Neighbors told investigators that Lambert knew them all, and would have felt comfortable running to any one of their homes should she have felt threatened, or if someone was following her.

A neighbor told investigators that she saw a green van with two men inside roaming around the neighborhood around the time of Lambert's disappearance.

Soon after Lambert disappeared, her mother received an anonymous phone call. A girl's voice told her "Mom, I'm OK", but her mother does not believe that it was really Lambert making the call.

The case grew cold, until a quarter of a century later in 2010, when a shocking confession would blow the case wide open. Detectives Sean M. Tice and Howard F. Cole

(Skip) decided to take a last concerted effort to solve the case, at the time the county's longest-running missing persons case.

They again interviewed family members, neighbors and acquaintances. Several of them told the detectives that they should take another look at David Lambert. He had always been a strong suspect in the investigation, but no evidence had ever been found to support an arrest.

Tice and Cole decided to try again. They interviewed him three separate times, for a total of over twenty hours. Showing him a photo of Lambert, they approached the interview by telling him it was all about getting justice for his sister.

David Lambert "tiptoed" up to giving a confession several times, but in the end he always withdrew. Eventually though, he cracked, and drew the detectives a map where he said they would find her body, along with a few lines of a confession. While he wrote the confession he was left in the interview room alone.

He picked up a piece of paper, wrote a careful word or line, put the pen down, and then thought again, laboring over his work. He worked on the map and confession so dedicatedly, detectives were sure that it was the real deal.

David confessed that he had walked with his sister down to the abandoned Florida Memorial College, which was at the corner of King Street and Holmes Boulevard. An argument broke out between the pair over a $20 bill.

He told investigators that Lambert had gotten angry and punched him. He pushed her away and she tripped and fell, impaling her head on a piece of steel. According to David Lambert, she died almost instantly.

David Lambert then told investigators that he screamed for

help, but at fourteen years old, when no one responded he panicked. He was also terrified of his parent's reaction, thinking that his parents would kill him in return.

He buried his sister's body in the woods, and then never said another word about any of it for twenty-five years.

When she was told of her son's confession, Lambert's mother refused to believe it. She continues to say that her son told police what they wanted to hear, and believes that the mystery men in a green van took her daughter all those years ago.

Investigators searched the woods for Lambert's remains, but none were found. It is however entirely possible that after twenty-five years and multiple redevelopment works done on the site, there was simply nothing left to find.

Current Status:
Most missing persons cases in the county are resolved within a few hours, or at the longest a few weeks. Until her brother's confession, Lambert's case was just one of three never solved.

David Lambert has not been charged because the time limit from the statute of limitations on manslaughter that was in effect in 1985 has expired. The State Attorney's Office has stated they made this decision after also taking into account David Lambert's age at the time of the offense, and other mitigating circumstances.

His confession to detectives Tice and Cole was not the first time he'd confessed to being involved in Lambert's death. When he was arrested for passing a bad check in 2000, he told police that he was responsible for Lambert's death, and named a different burial place.

However no body was found, nor was there any supporting evidence, and so charges were not filed.

Tice and Cole believe that with his confession, David Lambert can finally move on with his life. Until he told the truth in 2010, in their eyes he was still the same scared fourteen year old who buried his sister's body in the woods.

Victim: Diane Lee Maxwell Jackson
Location: Houston, Texas
Suspect: James Ray Davis
Date of Crime: December 14, 1969
Date of Conviction: November 24, 2003

Backstory:
Diane Lee Maxwell Jackson was born on May 12, 1944 in Louisiana to parents David M. and Nora Maxwell. Her brother David was 5 years her junior.

The twenty-five year old single mother lived at 5107 Belmont in Houston and worked as a Southern Bell telephone operator.

On The Day In Question:
On December 14, 1969, Maxwell was running late for work. She parked her car in the company parking lot, but never made it to her desk. Instead, she was forced into a nearby shack, where she was raped, and then strangled and stabbed to death.

Investigation:
Police investigated Maxwell's case, but no suspect was ever identified. Her car was fingerprinted and latent prints were lifted from it. When no match was found, the prints were filed away. The case went cold.

More than three decades later, Maxwell Jackson's brother, David Maxwell, pushed to have her case reopened. Working in law enforcement himself, he had started reviewing and working on his sister's case file himself in 1989. At that time he asked investigators to run the prints again, again no match was found.

Technology improved, and he asked again in 2003. This time, a match was made to James Ray Davis, who had never been a suspect before. He did have a criminal record, but had been released from prison ten years ago and as far as anyone could tell, he'd gotten his life back on the straight and narrow.

Identifying the prints was a huge job. They were first found stored incorrectly in archives from 1984. That search alone took a month. The prints were then run against the Houston Police's database, but as Davis had never been arrested in Houston there was no match to find in Houston's or the state's databases. Databases included only Davis's thumbprints.

The breakthrough came when the prints were run through the FBI's Integrated Automated Fingerprint Identification System (IAFIS). Prints are voluntarily submitted to the FBI by law enforcement agencies at the local, state, and federal level.

The FBI then categorizes the prints along with any criminal background linked to the individual. Law enforcement agencies can then request a search through IAFIS to identify prints found at crime scenes. The database contains over 70 million subjects.

When the latent prints from Maxwell Jackson's crime scene were run, IAFIS had only been online for three years. Within five hours it provided a list of twenty potential matches. A technician then examined that shortlist and found a definitive match with Davis's prints.

When they examined Davis's background, investigators discovered that he had only been released from prison for nine days when he killed Maxwell Jackson. Within a month of her murder he was already back in prison again, this time for auto theft.

Investigators located Davis living in federally funded housing on the Texas-Arkansas border. Arguably, anyone could have touched Maxwell Jackson's car on the day of her murder, and so they needed a confession.

Davis originally seemed calm and friendly, but after the homicide detectives asked him about his life in 1969 and 1970 and revealed they were from Houston, he became visibly shocked and nervous.

Davis confessed to killing Maxwell Jackson, but not to raping her. He was printed again and a DNA swab was also taken. He was released, but placed under surveillance until an arrest warrant could be issued. Davis chose to surrender himself at a parking lot a block away from where he lived.

On January 15, 2004, Davis pled guilty to Maxwell Jackson's murder. He was sentenced to life in prison.

Current Status:
Before her death, Maxwell Jackson's brother, David Maxwell, was planning on becoming a lawyer. After she died he changed his path in life and joined the Texas State Highway Patrol, and then the Texas Rangers. Would Maxwell Jackson's death forever have remained unsolved were it not for her brother's change in career choice?

Three Boys Gone

Victims: Robert Peterson, Anton Schuessler, and John Schuessler
Location: Chicago, Illinois
Suspect: Kenneth Hansen
Date of Crime: October 16, 1955
Date of Conviction: August 2002

Backstory:
Robert M. Peterson was born on February 11, 1942 to Malcolm and Dorothy Peterson. Little more is known about him other than he lived in the same neighborhood and was friends with the Schuessler boys.

John Schuessler was born on November 30, 1941 and Anton Jr. was born on November 12, 1943. Their parents were Anton Sr. and Eleanor Holz Schuessler Kujawa. Their father Anton Sr. died not long after his sons' deaths.

John was 13, his brother Anton Jr. was 11 and Robert was 14 years old when they died.

On The Day In Question:
On Sunday October 16, 1955, the three boys traveled together downtown. They were going to see a matinee of a Disney documentary movie, The African Lion. Back in the 1950s it was not unusual for children the boy's ages to be making the trip to the cinema without an adult. The three boys all had proven themselves to be responsible, and their parents trusted them to make the trip alone.

The boys had $4 to share between them, and were catching the train to the movies.

Strangely, the next sighting of the boys was at 6:00pm that evening, a long time after the movie screening had finished. The boys had been seen together in the Garland Building's lobby. Probably co-incidentally, Peterson's optometrists' office was in the same building, but the boys had no known reason for visiting.

The boys were next seen at the Monte Cristo Bowling Alley at 7:45pm. They left to go to a different bowling alley, and then tried to hitchhike at the corner of Lawrence and Milwaukee Avenue. It was now 9:05pm and their parents began to worry that they had not yet returned home.

No one saw any of the boys alive again.

Investigation:
The bowling alley owner told police that a man in his fifties was showing abnormal interest towards several young boys in the building, but he could not confirm whether the man had specifically had any interaction with the missing boys.

Two days passed, and the bodies of the Schuessler brothers and Peterson were found lying in a ditch near the Des Plaines River, in Robinson Woods Forest Preserve. They were discovered by a man who had pulled over to eat lunch.

After the autopsies the coroner ruled the cause death of all three boys was asphyxiation. Peterson had also been struck multiple times. By the time their bodies were found, they had already been dead for at least thirty-six hours.

Public fear and outrage over the deaths was high. People were horrified that three boys couldn't see a movie on a Sunday afternoon and travel home safely. Police officers searched the area, including questioning residents and searching every house in the neighborhood.

Teams also searched the entire woods, searching for evidence or clues of the killer's identity. Whoever had killed the boys had been extremely thorough in removing any traces. No fingerprints or trace evidence was found.

Unfortunately, the search and investigation was hampered by the arrival of multiple city and county police departments. There was next to no co-ordination or co-operation between the agencies, and evidence may have been lost or missed.

Murder does not have any statute of limitations, and so the case remained open. However as time passed any leads dried up and the case went cold.

Many years later, in 1994, a lead would come from the most unexpected of places. ATF agents investigating the disappearance of candy heiress Helen Vorhees Brach (her case is discussed in my book *Murders Unsolved*) when an informant named Kenneth Hansen as being involved in the murders of the three boys.

The informant told the investigators that Hansen had threatened others by saying that they would "end up like the Peterson boy". It turned out that the FBI had already been informed of this in the 1970's, but no one had ever looked into it. Could this information have helped to solve this case over two decades earlier?

When the boys went missing, Hansen had been twenty-two years old, and worked for Silas Jayne in his horse stables. Jayne was also implicated in Brach's disappearance and was suspected of multiple criminal dealings and violent interactions.

Perhaps Hansen could feel the investigation start to focus on him. He started asking neighbors if anyone had seen police around his home, and when he was arrested by Special Agent Jim Grady, it was discovered that he had a bag already packed and was ready to leave town.

Hansen was initially arrested for arson from a fire in 1972, and the same day was charged with the boys' murders.

Prosecutors argued that Hansen had taken the boys back to the stables where he worked and sexually abused at least one of them, before killing them all. Hansen dumped their bodies and when Jayne discovered what he'd done, the stables were burned down to destroy any remaining evidence.

Hansen was convicted in 1995, but the conviction was overturned on appeal five years later.

In 2002 he went to trial again and was again found guilty. Hansen was sentenced to 200-300 years in jail.

Current Status:
1,200 people attended the boys' funeral.

Kenneth Hansen continued to protest his innocence. He died in prison in 2007.

Victims: Richard A. Phillips and Milton Curtis
Location: El Segundo, California
Suspect: G.D. Wilson /Gerald F. Mason
Date of Crime: July 22, 1957
Date of Conviction: March 24, 2003

Backstory:
According to statistics, Los Angeles is the most dangerous place in the United States to be a police officer. Nearly every day of the year in Los Angeles, a police officer is shot in the line of duty.

In 1957, Officers Richard Phillips and Milton Curtis were both police officers at the El Segundo Police Department, a city in Los Angeles County, California.

Richard A. Phillips was born on September 10, 1928 in Muskogee, Oklahoma. He and his wife Carole had three children, Carolyn, Patricia and Richard Jr. He had been a police officer for about 2 years.

Milton G. Curtis was born on January 30, 1932 in Arizona. He had only been an El Segundo police officer for 2 months when he was killed. He was survived by his wife Jean and two children, son Keith and daughter Toni.

On The Day In Question:
It was July 22, 1957. That evening had been a violent one in town. A man had come across four teenagers at a local "lovers lane". After forcing them to strip to their underwear, he raped one of the girls, and then fled the scene in the teen's car.

When he ran a red light, he was pulled over by the Officers Phillips and Curtis. At that time, the officers had no idea what the man had just done, and treated it as a routine traffic stop.

A second police car with two fellow officers passed by while they were starting the traffic stop, but Officer Phillips indicated that all was fine and the second unit kept driving. Within moments after they left the scene they heard over the radio that their fellow officers had been shot.

This was 1957, and police cars did not have dash cameras. When fellow officers arrived on the scene they found Curtis already dead, sitting in the patrol car. Phillips was lying on the ground, and was still alive, but mortally wounded by three shots in his back. Medical personnel arrived with the backup, but both officers died as a result of their wounds.

In the short time it took first responders to arrive at the scene, the car that Phillips and Curtis had pulled over disappeared.

Investigation:
The murder of a police officer always invokes a strong response. But when this one occurred, the early investigation was hampered by one major oversight. At that time, there was no report of the stolen car, and so police did not know what they were looking for.

The teenagers had not yet reported the theft. They would soon after be found walking the streets, near naked and terrified. By the time they reported the crime against them, officers were already swarming the murder scene. Perhaps if they'd known about the attack on the teens earlier, they could have put the two together and started looking for the stolen car.

The car was eventually found dumped and empty. One of the first officers on the scene acting as a crime scene investigator was Howard Speaks. He noticed that there were bullet holes all over the car. There were holes in the trunk, and two in the rear windshield, which shattered it.

He noted that only two rounds were found inside the car. Had Officer Phillips managed to actually hit the perpetrator?

To this day officers are amazed at how the rounds must have gotten there. Officer Phillips was an excellent marksman, but managing to get off six rounds at the fleeing car, hitting it three times, all while he lay dying, was incredible.

The car was thoroughly searched, looking for possible evidence. In 1957 there was no such thing as DNA collection, but fingerprints were taken.

One of the teens taken hostage was able to give a good description of the man. He was described as being around six feet tall, about two hundred pounds, with short hair. He mentioned that the man had a peculiar way of holding his head, and appeared frightened but arrogant.

In 1960, a man doing yard work found a gun in his backyard. The man lived less than a mile from the scene of the police officer's murders. He handed it in to police, and it was identified as the murder weapon of Phillips and Curtis. Investigators traced the gun back to Shreveport, Louisiana.

It had been bought at a sporting goods store in 1957. Store records showed a single name G.D. Wilson. Local records at a YMCA showed a George D. Wilson, but after checking every George Wilson in the county, they found no fingerprint match to the scene. Was the name G.D. Wilson simply an alias?

Despite the physical evidence and description from the teen victims, no suspect had emerged, and the case went cold. It would stay that way for nearly fifty years.

Then, in 2002, police received a new lead out of the blue. A woman called the police department and told them that an uncle had bragged about killing two El Segundo police officers. Out of nowhere, they had a name.

The first thing the police did was to try and match the prints from 1957. Experts from the Los Angeles Sheriff's Department, Dale Falicon and Don Keir, did the tests. They could tell immediately that the prints did not match the new suspect.

They weren't beat yet. Using the advantage of modern technology, they were able to digitally reprocess the original crime scene photographs with computer technology that wasn't even dreamt of in the 1950s. This gave them a fingerprint that could be run through the modern day databases.

They ran the new digitally enhanced fingerprints through the FBI's nation-wide criminal database. They found a match. His name was Gerald F. Mason. Mason had only one record in the system, for a burglary in 1956 in South Carolina. He had no criminal record from before the murder of the officers or since.

Remarkably, Mason was found still living with his family in his hometown. He was now a retiree. Could this old man who was pushing seventy, with barely a criminal record, possibly be a brutal and cold-blooded rapist and cop killer?

Police engaged a document examiner expert. He compared the handwriting of George D. Wilson from a YMCA sign-in receipt to Mason's handwriting. It was practically identical.

On January 29, 2003, Mason opened his front door to find a large group of police officers standing on his stoop. Shocked, he asked them where they were from. When he was told they were from Los Angeles, his response was that he thought he needed a lawyer.

When he was searched after his arrest, it was found that Mason had a bullet graze scar across his back. It seemed that Officer Phillips had indeed found his mark.

Confronted with the evidence against him, Mason pled guilty and was sentenced to two consecutive life terms in prison.

Current Status:
Curtis's widow was only twenty-three when he died. She says she has never really gotten over his death.

Mason told police that he originally bought the gun for protection, as he was planning to hitchhike from Louisiana. He had no answer as to why he attacked the teens, but he shot the police officers as a result of a split second decision to avoid being caught for his first crime.

After the murder of the two officers, Mason led a life as a law-abiding citizen. He did not even get a parking ticket. When he was sentenced, he gave a tearful apology to the victim's families. Police believe that he was just sorry to have been caught.

Mason became eligible for parole in 2009, but it was denied. He is next eligible to apply in 2017. Prosecutors vow that he will never be released.

Three Little Girls Delayed Justice

Victims: Christi Meeks, Christie Proctor and Roxann Reyes
Location: Northern Texas, United States
Suspect: David Elliot Penton
Dates of Crimes: January 1985, February 1986 & November 1987
Date of Conviction: 2005

Backstory:
Christi Lynn Meeks was born June 21, 1979 to parents Michael and Linda. She had a brother Michael, a sister and one stepbrother. Her parents were divorced and both remarried. Christi lived with her father Michael and his wife Lisa. Her mother Linda had married Edwin Peacock and they had a son together.

Christie Dianne Proctor was born Christie Dianne Sherrill on February 29, 1976 to parents Howard and Laura Sherrill. She was an only child. After their divorce in 1977, her mother Laura remarried Cooper L. Proctor and Christie's name was changed to Proctor.

Roxann Hope Reyes born January 14, 1984 to Sergio Reyes and Tamela Osborne. She too was an only child. After Roxann's death, her mother Tamela divorced Sergio Reyes and married Jesus A. Lopez.

In the 1980's multiple murders of small girls occurred in Texas. All three girls had been grabbed, assaulted, and then strangled to death. Christi Meeks was 5 and from Mesquite, Christie Proctor, 9, from Dallas, and Roxann Reyes from Garland, who was just days away from her fourth birthday at the time of her death.

On The Day In Question:
Police believed that all three girls had been abducted and then killed by someone who was a stranger to them. Their

families endured months of not knowing what happened to their daughters, as investigators searched for the missing girls. Unfortunately, only their dead bodies were found.

Meeks had been playing hide and seek outside her home, a Mesquite apartment complex, when she disappeared on January 19, 1985. Her body was found in Lake Texoma almost three months later on April 3.

Proctor was last seen walking from her parents' apartment in North Dallas to a friend's house on February 15, 1986. It would be more than two years before her body was recovered from a field in Plano, Texas in April 1988.

Reyes was taken from an alley while she was playing outside her parents' apartment on November 3, 1987. It was six months before her body was found in Murphy, Texas in May 1988.

Investigation:
Although police were disturbed by the kidnappings and killings, none of the girls' deaths had any significant leads or suspects identified.

In 1996, the girls' cases caught the attention of a police detective in Garland, Gary Sweet. Along with the case files, the name of a suspect caught his eye, David Elliot Penton. There were many pages of evidence and documentation within the files, but for some reason Penton's name caught Detective Sweet's eye. Perhaps it was fate.

At that time, Penton was already in jail in Ohio for the murder of a nine-year-old girl. Detectives made multiple trips between the two states, but were unable to tie Penton to the Texas murders.

In 2000, Sweet received a phone call from a detective from Fort Worth. The detective had received a letter from an inmate in an Ohio prison regarding a child homicide in Ohio. In the letter, the inmate names his cellmate as the killer, and also said that the cellmate told him he was responsible for killing a girl from Garland named Roxann Reyes.

The detective from Fort Worth invited Sweet along to a phone interview with the cellmate, scheduled for the next day. The inmate's cellmate was David Elliot Penton.

The next day, Sweet questioned the inmate regarding Reyes' murder, and he correctly reported many details of the case, including what the victim was wearing. The inmate could only talk for ten minutes so Sweet left his own contact details with him.

The Forth Worth detective set up a meeting with every law enforcement agency in Texas who had dealt with the disappearance or murder of a child from 1984-1988. The agencies were invited to come together to compare notes on their cases. Sweet attended the meeting, and was surprised by the sheer number of cases of missing children in Texas.

After the meeting, the detectives in Fort Worth tested the DNA from their case against Penton's. A few days later they informed Sweet that his DNA did not match their case. They surmised that their contact was unreliable, and stopped talking to the inmate. Something bothered Sweet and he kept contact open with the inmate.

After talking to the inmate again, Sweet requested a copy of the letter be sent to Forth Worth police. The inmate had not actually said that Penton had killed the Forth Worth victim, but suggested that he should be a suspect in Reyes' murder. The inmate believed that Penton had only bragged about the Fort Worth murder, but his confessions regarding Reyes were the real deal.

The inmate had researched the cases on his own, and based on his own experiences with Penton, believed that it was very possible he was the perpetrator of Reyes' murder, even though he may have taken credit for others he had not committed.

Along with others he named, he insisted that Penton must be Reyes' killer because he knew her full name, and many other details about Reyes and the case. Along with Reyes, the inmate also listed Meeks and Proctor as definite victims.

Meanwhile, other law enforcement officers told Sweet that his inmate informant was known not to be trustworthy. They also found out that he had filed open record requests and had received open records on the cases he'd spoken to Sweet about.

The investigator working with Sweet decided to stop talking to the informant, but again Sweet felt he had to keep contact open, even though he did not know why.

When asked why he pulled the open records, the inmate told Sweet that when you lived in a 12x12 cell all day with a man who talks about nothing but killing children, he had to know whether or not he was telling the truth.

Sweet followed up on what the inmate had actually received, and found out that he hadn't actually gotten all the records he requested, including the file on Reyes' murder. The inmate also did not have access to the Internet or any other way to get the information.

Therefore, he couldn't have gotten any of the details he'd told Sweet from any place but Penton. Was it possible that his reports about Penton were true?

Later, the inmate gave Detective Sweet the name of a girl that Penton had allegedly kidnapped in Dallas, but then let go. Penton had told him that he'd been hired by the girl's father to scare her, but neither the inmate nor Sweet believed that.

Sweet found the girl living in Mississippi and made contact. After confirming she was the true victim by corroborating details from the original police report, she dropped a bombshell on Sweet, telling him that just three days later the same man that took her kidnapped a girl from her school. That girl was not so lucky. Her name was Christie Proctor.

This new victim had been abducted from the same place as Proctor. Could she place Penton at the scene of the crime at the same time as Proctor's abduction? The victim had previously been involved in creating a composite of her kidnapper, but it did not look much like Penton.

Sweet continued to work the case on his own time, as well as working his usual caseload. In his files he found a statement that had been taken from Penton's sister. She told investigators that she never wanted to be around him again, and did not want him having any contact with her children.

She believed her brother was responsible for the murders of all three girls in Texas. He noticed that Penton's sister lived in Oklahoma, Texas, and that Penton would visit his sister. They could now place Penton in Oklahoma.

Sweet contacted authorities and one of the Oklahoma detectives had actually been called out on the Meeks case before transferring to Oklahoma. They joined the investigation, followed by a detective from Plano, Texas. Sweet later reported that the extra manpower made all the difference to the investigation.

Sweet was still talking to the informant, who tells him that Penton told him that if he ever wanted to hide something, put it in the ceiling in the insulation, as the cops will never want to get all dirty searching up there.

The investigators again searched the home where Penton lived when growing up in Columbus. Other evidence, including little girls panties, had previously been found, but none of the finds could be linked to either Penton or any victims.

Up in the roof, under some boards that had been placed over the rafters, they found a big bundle of rags tied up in yarn. At first they thought the bundle would contain evidence, but when it was opened the detectives discovered that it was just a bunch of old rags. Noting some discolorations and stains on them however, they decided to have them tested by the lab.

It took up to year and a half to test all the samples. Tests revealed that semen, blood, and saliva were all found on the rags, but time and the exposure to the elements meant that the samples had degraded. Lab technicians could neither confirm nor deny that any of the DNA matched Penton or any of the girls.

Despite the evidence they were collecting, Sweet and his team decided to wait to interview Penton. According to Sweet, Penton was a pathological liar, and they did not want to approach him until they were sure they could prove the case.

The detectives made five trips to Ohio to interview people related to Penton. On the fifth trip, they made plans to interview Penton himself.

At the time of the interview, other members of the team would be searching his cell. For some time, with co-operation with prison investigators, the team had been receiving copies of all mail Penton sent and received.

Finding their own names in his correspondence, they realized that Penton knew they were looking at him. He had never seen any of the detectives, but the prison grapevine had let him know he was being investigated.

When they first introduced themselves to Penton in the Ohio prison, his face went white and Sweet reports that Penton lost track of his bodily functions. Penton was allegedly almost scared to death by their talk of application for extradition and the attitude in Texas towards the death penalty.

Using their understanding of Penton's personality, the detectives started the interview by praising how long it took them to find him and stroked his ego. They combined that with telling Penton they were not investigating him, they just wanted to meet him before he was extradited to Texas to face the death penalty.

When detectives mentioned the rags found in the attic in the Columbus house, Penton said "…but I never took any souvenirs". Sweet realized that this was just about a confession. When he later said that the finding of the rags was a lie, because he never left any physical evidence behind, Sweet called him on it, asking him if that meant he'd used a condom. Penton started rapidly backpedaling, saying he meant he didn't leave any physical evidence because he was not the one who had killed the girls.

Sweet reports that after his interview with Penton, any lingering doubt he had that he was the true killer was gone. The next day, the other detectives also interviewed Penton, and he continued to slip up a couple more times.

However, he never admitted anything outright, and technology at the time made recording the interviews difficult. Sweet hoped that the testimony of the four detectives in the room against Penton's would be enough.

Sweet and his team were determined to see the trial through to the end. However, prosecutors approached them and told Sweet he was worried about work records, one of which could place Penton out of state at the time of one of the murders. The prosecution was worried that if one murder were refuted, it would affect all the others.

Prosecutors approached Penton's lawyers and offered to remove the death penalty from the table if Penton pled guilty. They felt it was better to guarantee he would be in prison for the rest of his life, rather than go to trial and have him potentially go free.

After Penton's guilty plea was accepted, Sweet found out some time later that Penton's job where the timecard placed him out of state was for doing the timecards for that business. It would have been extremely easy for him to falsify his own record. He claims they did not have time to investigate that before the guilty plea was entered.

Current Status:
David Penton claims that he is innocent of the murders of the three girls, and only pled guilty to avoid the death penalty and create time for someone to listen to his claims of innocence. He also claims he did not want to drag his family through a murder trial.

He blames the deaths on a Jordanian national who allegedly fled the country before authorities could interview him. However, he does admit that if he had been on a jury for his own trial, he would have found himself guilty.

Penton has allegedly told his cellmate he is responsible for at least twenty other murders. One inmate told investigators that Penton said once he had raped a girl, they would just be a burden on society and of no other use, so why not kill them and throw them away. Sweet believes that Penton is a psychopath and has no conscious or soul.

Multiple members of the girls' families were not happy with Penton's plea bargain. Prosecutors had told them from the beginning that they would be seeking the death penalty. They cited that evidence that Penton was out of state the day Reyes was abducted could have hurt their case, and that was why they accepted the plea.

Penton will be eligible for parole in Ohio in 2027, at which time if he is freed he will be transferred to Texas to serve three life sentences.

Penton has involvement, or suspected involvement, in multiple other crimes. He has also been convicted of involuntary manslaughter after he shook his infant son to death in 1985.

Two of his ex-wives have reported that he sexually abused their children. Investigators believe he may be responsible for the deaths of up to fifty children.

Detective Sweet said that in the end Penton's downfall was that he liked to talk. As well as the original informant, several other inmates have also come forward and corroborated his claims, telling investigators stories that Penton allegedly told them also. Many inmates told Sweet that they were surprised that it took so long for police to catch up with him.

Legos Were The Final Clue

Victim: Lucille Johnson
Location: Holladay, Utah
Suspect: John Sansing
Date of Crime: February 1, 1991
Date of Conviction: August 2014

Backstory:
Lucille Johnson was a grandmother from Holladay, Utah. In 1991 she was seventy-eight years old, and lived on her own in a mobile home.

She was a small woman, at 4'11" tall and weighed just one hundred and twenty-two pounds.

Her family describes her as very tender and loving, with lots of energy, despite her age. Her daughter has said that she brought many blessings into others' lives.

On The Day In Question:
On February 1, 1991, Johnson was seen sweeping her porch. Later, when her family couldn't reach her, her daughter went to her home to check on her. She found her mother's body.

Investigation:
Johnson was left lying in bed, and had been brutally beaten. As well as a fractured skull, all of Johnson's ribs were broken. An autopsy showed that the cause of death was strangulation.

When they first entered the home, police officers were surprised to find Lego toys littered around on the living room floor. Family members told them that Johnson kept them on hand for her grandchildren, but she never would have left them lying about on the floor. They also discovered that a necklace and ring were missing.

Tissue samples were taken from underneath Johnson's nails, but at the time of her death the technology for testing the DNA wasn't yet available.

From the beginning, police suspected the killer was someone Johnson knew. There was no sign of forced entry, and her daughter reported the doors had been locked when she arrived to check on her mom.

Despite investigator's best efforts however, the case went cold. Salt Lake City Sheriff's investigators continued to work on the case until 2006, when a lack of any new leads forced them to stop any investigation.

In 2013, twenty-three years after Johnson's death, the case was re-opened. Technology had advanced to the point that the scrapings that had been collected from under Johnson's nails all those years ago could be tested for DNA. They were run and a match was found, a man named John Sansing. Sansing was identified because his DNA profile was in the database due to another violent crime he'd committed. In fact, he was already on death row for a similar murder.

Disturbingly, when investigators re-tested the strangely scattered Lego blocks for fingerprints, they found they matched Sansing's son. At the time of Johnson's death, he had been just five years old. Sansing had left him playing with the Lego blocks while he murdered Johnson in the next room.

In August 2014, Sansing was charged with the first-degree felony murder of Johnson. Contrary to their earlier beliefs that Johnson knew her killer, investigators don't believe that she knew Sansing at all.

Current Status:
Sansing's son has since told investigators that he remembers accompanying his father to Johnson's house,

and the memories had traumatized him for two decades. Sansing had allegedly also taken his son to the murder that he was already in jail for.

After Sansing's DNA was matched, his wife came forward and admitted to detectives that he had told her in 1991 that he'd killed an elderly lady in Holladay. His nephew also told police that he had overhead Sansing and his wife arguing, with her threatening him that she'd tell police about the murdered woman in Utah. He reportedly physically abused his wife, but others say that her culture (she had grown up in Bangladesh) would have prevented her from leaving him.

The Salt Lake County Sherriff is quoted as saying he believes Sansing is simply evil. Sansing is in an Arizona prison on death row for an unrelated murder.

A Mother Exonerated

Victim: Azaria Chamberlain
Location: Northern Territory, Australia
Suspects: Lindy and Michael Chamberlain
Date of Death: August 17, 1980
Case Closed Date: June 12, 2012

Backstory:
The case of the death of Azaria Chamberlain is possibly the most notorious trial and verdict in Australia's history. Azaria was just nine weeks old when she disappeared from her family's campsite in Australia's Northern Territory on August 17, 1980.

Her disappearance and assumed death (her body has never been recovered) divided the nation, and has inspired multiple TV specials and also a movie starring Meryl Streep.

Azaria Chamberlain was born June 11, 1980 to Lindy and Michael Chamberlain. The pair was married November 18, 1969 and lived in Tasmania for about five years. They also had two older boys, Aidan and Reagan who were 7 and 4 in 1980. The family had moved to Mount Isa in Northern Queensland in Australia.

On The Day In Question:
Azaria's family, including her mother Lindy and father Michael, and her two older siblings, were camping near Uluru, known at the time as Ayers Rock. Azaria Chamberlain had been put to bed in a cot in the tent, while the rest of her family remained nearby. It was later in the night when Lindy Chamberlain's now well known cries split the air – "A dingo's got my baby!"

Investigation:
The first investigations seemed to support the Chamberlain's claims that a dingo had taken Azaria. Other

people at the campsite reported hearing growling shortly before Lindy Chamberlain's cries were heard.

Paw prints were found at the door of the tent, and drag marks were found in the sand. Canine hairs were found in the tent, and Lindy Chamberlain told police she had seen a dingo leave the tent.

A first inquest into Chamberlain's death was held in December of 1980, and was the first to be telecast live across Australia. The magistrate ruled that the likely cause of death was a dingo attack, but believed that the body of Chamberlain had been taken from the dingo and disposed of by persons unknown.

Many Australians did not believe the verdict, and were suspicious of the Chamberlains. The Northern Territory police and prosecutors were also unsatisfied, and continued to investigate the case, despite the coronial inquest's ruling.

The Chamberlains were Seventh-day Adventists, a religion that at the time was not well understood in Australia. Rumors began to circulate, including the claim that the baby's unusual name of Azaria means "sacrifice in the wildernesses". This is untrue, but even today some still believe it.

A second inquest was held in September of 1981. This time a forensic expert from the UK testified that using ultraviolet photographs he was able to determine that there was an incised wound around the neck of the jumpsuit. He claimed this indicated that someone had slit Chamberlain's throat. He also claimed that there was a small adult's handprint on the jumpsuit.

A forensic biologist then testified that blood had been found in the Chamberlain's car, on a camera bag in the car, and on a pair of scissors. She also claimed that there was blood on the handprint on the jumpsuit.

The case went to trial, the prosecution alleging that Lindy Chamberlain slit her baby's throat with the scissors, and then hid her body in the camera bag. She then allegedly rejoined the camping group and fed her other children, before going to the tent to raise the alarm. Finally, it was alleged that she snuck the body away while the others were out searching for the baby.

Lindy Chamberlain claimed that Azaria had been wearing a matinee jacket over the jumpsuit, but the jacket was now missing. Evidence in her defense included eyewitness testimony that multiple dingoes were seen nearby that evening. A nurse who was present also testified to hearing a baby's cry after the time that prosecutors alleged she was already dead.

A forensic test found fetal hemoglobin in the Chamberlain's car. Fetal hemoglobin is found in babies up to 6 months old and Azaria, being only 9 weeks old, certainly would have still had it in her blood.

Experts testified that other substances such as adult blood, mucus, and even chocolate milkshakes, could all test positive for fetal hemoglobin with the test that was used. Both of the latter two substances were in the car at the time of Chamberlain's death.

An engineer testified that contrary to widespread popular opinion, a dingo's teeth could sheer through fabric easily, and was also strong enough to carry a baby. In fact, just weeks earlier a three year old child had been removed from a car seat by a dingo, the event witnessed by her parents. However, this evidence was mostly ignored.

Some people believed that state resources were being used to prosecute two people unjustly, but the

Chamberlains also faced incredible hostility from the general public. As far as most people were concerned, they were guilty before even being tried.

The press was voracious, seizing on anything to sensationalize the trial. They claimed that Lindy Chamberlain often dressed Azaria in black. It was in fact a fashion of the time to have dark clothing with bright colored accents, but it was seen as negative.

Claims were made that the Seventh-day Adventist church was actually a cult that sacrificed infants. Lindy Chamberlain herself, likely in shock and suffering from grief, showed little emotion during the proceedings, a fact that was also used against her.

Many newspapers also published cartoons and editorial pieces condemning the family. People also petitioned outside the court wearing shirts that read "The dingo is innocent".

Lindy Chamberlain was found guilty of murder and sentenced to life in prison. Michael Chamberlain was found guilty as an accessory after the fact, and was given a suspended sentence.

An appeal was made to quash the convictions to the High Court of Australia in November of 1983, but it was refused.

In 1986, a random discovery turned the case on its head. An English tourist who had been climbing Uluru fell. Because of the rock's enormous size, and the scrub surrounding the base, it was over a week before his body was found.

His body was resting below the bluff from which he had fallen, an area that was full of dingoes. Police were searching the area for the tourist's bones that may have been carried off by dingoes when they found a small piece of clothing – a baby's matinee jacket.

The jacket was soon identified as the missing jacket from Chamberlain's case, and the Chief Minister of the Northern Territory ordered Chamberlain's immediate release from prison. Azaria Chamberlain's case was officially re-opened.

It has since been discovered that the forensic evidence that had convicted the Chamberlains was extremely questionable. The test that showed blood in the car and on the items had been only a presumptive test, and had not been confirmed that it truly was blood. In fact, it had shown positive because of the presence of copper oxide.

The Chamberlains lived in Mt. Isa, Queensland, a mining town where the material was common. It was also shown that a sound deadener that was sprayed during the manufacture of the Chamberlain's car also tested positive for fetal hemoglobin, and in fact the scientific community knew the test was wildly unreliable.

In a later royal commission, the UK expert also testified that he had only assumed the handprint on the jacket had been in blood. He had never even tested it.

On September 15, 1988, the Chamberlain's convictions were unanimously overturned in the court of appeals. Two years later, they were awarded $1.3 million in Australian compensation. This did not make them rich, in fact it only covered a third of their incurred legal expenses.

In 1995, a third inquest into Chamberlain's death was held, but despite the evidence that now existed, it returned an open finding, meaning that the cause of death was unknown.

Finally in 2012, a fourth and final inquest ruled that Chamberlain had been taken from her cot and killed by a dingo. There were both tears and loud applause from the court gallery when the verdict was read.

Current Status:
Today the overwhelming majority of Australians believe the Chamberlains were always innocent. In fact, a motive could never be found to explain why Lindy Chamberlain would have committed the crime.

Azaria Chamberlain's case was the first unprovoked dingo attack that became widely known. Back then it was believed that dingoes would not approach humans and would not attack unless provoked.

Since Chamberlain's death, there have been multiple dingo attacks against children in Australia, including one causing the death of a nine-year-old boy in 2001. It is now known that dingoes can and will attack unprovoked.

The Chamberlains have since divorced, and have both remarried. They believe that had Azaria's death and the circus of a trial not occurred, they would still be together.

At the final inquest, the magistrate formally apologized to the family. Lindy Chamberlain wrapped her arms around her son, who was six at the time of Azaria's death, and they both wept together as the verdict was read.

Brown's Chicken Murders

Victims: Richard Ehlenfeldt, Lynn Ehlenfeldt, Guadalupe Maldonado, Michael Castro, Rico Solis, Thomas Mennes, Marcus Nellsen
Location: Chicago, Illinois
Suspects: James Degorski and Juan Luna
Date of Crime: January 8, 1993
Dates of Conviction: May 10, 2007 and September 29, 2009

Backstory:
Brown's Chicken is a popular restaurant franchise based in Chicago, Illinois. In 1949 John and Belva Brown opened the first Brown's Chicken restaurant. By the 1970's, the franchise had grown to include many restaurants around the United States.

Pasta was added to the menu in the 1980's and Brown's Chicken became Brown's Chicken and Pasta. After 2005, the franchise limited its restaurants to the Chicago area.

On The Day In Question:
On January 8, 1993, the day started as usual at Brown's Chicken in Palatine, a suburb of Chicago. Then, later that night just before closing, a man ran into the store. He was armed and yelled for everyone to get down on the floor.

Seven people were killed that night, the two owners and five staff members. Their bodies were then piled into the freezer. It was more than five hours after closing time before police discovered their bodies.

Investigation:
The first report that something might be wrong at the shop came when the parents of Michael Castro, the sixteen-year-old cook, called police several hours after the 9:00pm closing time.

The wife of another staff member, Guadalupe Maldonado, also called police. She was anxious that her husband had not returned home, and that his car was still in the Brown's Chicken parking lot.

After her call, police visited the building and discovered that the rear door was open. When they entered the building they found the staff members' dead bodies.

Less than $2,000 cash had been taken from the restaurant. More than two dozen shots had been fired, and so the perpetrators would have had to reload their weapons at least once.

Some of the victims were left alive for some time after watching colleagues die next to them. As well as dying from being shot, one victim's throat was also slit.

DNA was collected from the crime scene from a half-eaten piece of chicken. DNA testing was in its infancy at the time of the crime. However, police kept the chicken preserved in the hope that technology would advance to the point it could be useful.

A taskforce was formed, consisting of more than sixty members from multiple police agencies. Together they investigated thousands of leads. Just one day after the crime a former employee of the restaurant was arrested. He was released two days later.

On January 15, another five men were arrested. All except one were quickly released, the last being held on unrelated charges.

By January 25, a reward of $100,000 had been offered.

In July, relatives of the victims hung signs in the window of the restaurant, asking who had killed seven people. It would then be March 1994 before there was another arrest. That man too was released.

Another year passed, and Brown's Chicken re-opened at a new location. Around the same time, police asked former FBI investigator James F. Bell to work on the case. Bell had previously worked on the cases of several serial killers, including Ted Bundy.

Little progress was made, and by the time another year had passed there were now just seven people still working on the taskforce. The case had grown cold.

In March of 2002, police received a tip from a woman named Anne Lockett. She reported that an ex-boyfriend named James Degorski, along with an associate named Juan Luna, had committed the robbery and murders.

When police looked for a link, they discovered that Luna was a previous employee of Brown's Chicken.

Then came the clincher, thanks to the forward thinking crime scene technician who had saved the partially eaten chicken. Although it was impossible when the crime had been committed, she had foreseen a day when saliva could be tested for DNA.

Now in 2002, it was possible. Police tested the sample and got a match. Luna had been in the store that night.

Police arrested both men on May 16, 2002. The case went to trial, and both men pled not guilty. As well as the DNA evidence, the prosecution presented other evidence, including a partial palm print, and a taped confession that Luna had given police on May 17, the day after his arrest.

In it, he described the murders in gruesome detail. He had known from working there that there were no alarms on the back door, and where the safe would be. They attacked just a few minutes before closing, when he knew there would be few, if any, customers in the store.

In his confession, Luna also told police that they "walked funny" to avoid creating any footprint evidence as they left the scene. They also wore latex gloves to avoid leaving fingerprint evidence. Little did they know that Luna's impromptu chicken dinner would be their eventual downfall.

On May 10, 2007, after eleven hours deliberation, a jury convicted Luna of all charges. He was not given the death penalty. A single female juror refused to vote for it, and as it requires a unanimous decision, he received life in prison.

On September 29, 2009, Degorski was also found guilty and sentenced to life in prison, after less than two hours deliberation by the jury. In his case, there was no physical evidence.

He was convicted solely on statements made to police by his ex-girlfriend, as well as his own interview. Two jurors refused to vote on the death penalty in his case.

Current Status:
It was revealed in 2015 that Richard Zuley, a detective who served on the investigative task force was on a special assignment in 2003 as an interrogator of terrorism suspects at Guantanamo Bay.

Several suspects from various investigations throughout his career as a police officer have claimed that he used techniques such as shackling them to walls for extended periods, and coercing confessions by threatening family members. He is now the defendant in at least one pending lawsuit. Zuley retired from the police force in 2007.

The employee who was initially arrested was since cleared of all suspicion. He sued the city of Palatine for wrongful arrest. The case was settled in 1997.

The victim's families were, for the most part, pleased with the verdict. Several of them were vocal against the death penalty. Other family members of the victims felt strongly the other way, saying that when seven people were brutally killed just life in prison was not justice.

The restaurant building was razed in 2001, and in its place there is now a bank. The murders had a detrimental effect on the Brown's Chicken franchise as a whole. Business dropped by 35% in all restaurants, and eventually one hundred were closed across the Chicago area.

In March 2014, Degorski was awarded $451,000 compensation and punitive damages, after a jury found that he had been beaten to the point of requiring surgery by a sheriff in Cook County Jail in 2002. The deputy was fired.

A Halloween Mystery Solved

Victim: Shauna Howe
Location: Oil City, Pennsylvania
Suspects: Eldred 'Ted' Walker, James O'Brien, Timothy O'Brien
Date of Crime: October 27, 1992
Date of Conviction: October 25, 2005

Backstory:
Shauna Melinda Howe was born July 11, 1981 in Oil City, Pennsylvania to parents Lucy & Robert Howe. She was eleven years old, and lived with her mother in Oil City, Pennsylvania. She had brown hair and blue eyes, and was described as shy.

On The Day In Question:
On October 27, 1992, Howe was walking home from a Girl Scouts Halloween Party. She was dressed as a gymnast. Before the party, she and her fellow Girl Scouts had sung for the residents of an old age home.

She left the party, held at a local church, around 8:00pm. When she hadn't arrived home by 10:00pm, her mother called the police.

It was noted that police had also received a call several hours earlier, where a witness reported seeing a tall man snatch a little girl off the street. He appeared unkempt, and had forced the girl into a rust colored car. Had the witness seen Howe's abduction or were the police dealing with two child abductions on the same night?

Howe was less than two blocks from her home when she was abducted.

Investigation:
Police continued to search, joined by FBI agents and civilian volunteers, but no sign of Howe was found. Two

days after she disappeared one of Howe's family members found part of her costume, a leotard belonging to Howe's mother, lying on a hiking trail that was about eight miles from town. It was a day later when searchers found Howe's body.

Howe was found three days after her disappearance, lying face down at the bottom of a railroad trestle. She was wedged between a rock and a log in a dry creek bed, and had fallen thirty feet. An autopsy revealed that she had been alive when she had landed in the creek bed.

She had a dislocated shoulder and broken arm, indicating that Howe may have tried to break her fall. She also had fractured ribs that were poking through her chest. The coroner reported that although her cause of death was likely injuries from the fall, it was impossible to say whether she fell, was thrown, or had been forced to jump. He did say however that Howe could have lain injured for up to half an hour before she eventually succumbed to her injuries.

Both the local police and the FBI were involved in the case, and followed up on many leads, both local and some that came from as far away as Canada. No suspect was ever identified. By the time the New Year came, authorities were no closer to solving the case, and the rumor mill had started. Many locals believed that Howe's family had been involved in her death.

As the months passed with no arrest, the once peaceful community changed. Locked doors became common, and self-defense classes for children were offered. Children hardly ever traveled anywhere alone.

By the time Halloween rolled around again the next year, trick or treating was officially curtailed to just a couple of hours in the afternoon while the sun was still up. The next year, it continued that way and would for years.

In 1997, police hoped they might have a break in the case. Tragically, another local girl named Shenee Freeman, who was just four years old, went outside to play and was never seen alive again. A seventeen-year-old young man, who had joined the search party for Freeman, was later arrested and charged with her rape and murder.

Police hoped that he had also been responsible for Howe's kidnapping and death, but he could not be connected to the case. The teen pled guilty to Freeman's rape and murder and received a life sentence.

It was another ten years before investigators finally received the break they'd been waiting for. In 2002, a DNA sample was taken from a man, James O'Brien, who was in prison for attempted kidnapping in Oil City in 1995. His victim had been a grown woman.

Around the same time, police still investigating Howe's case had revisited a possible suspect, a local, Eldred 'Ted' Walker. He had been originally interviewed in 1992 but had not been arrested. Pressure on Walker was intensified and his home was searched. Walker eventually told police that he'd been involved with some "really bad" people back then.

Then came the kicker – the DNA taken from O'Brien in 2002 matched DNA found from a semen sample on Howe's leotard.

Walker eventually confessed that he had been the one to grab Howe, but it had all been part of a prank he had planned with James O'Brien and his brother Timothy, aimed at making the town's police look foolish.

Originally they had planned to kidnap a boy they knew, but they decided in the end that the kidnapping of a girl would get more attention. Selecting Howe as their victim had been a crime of opportunity, they had simply seen her walking home and grabbed her.

They drove her to Walker's home, and the O'Briens then took her upstairs. Walker claimed that when he discovered they were raping the girl he threw them out of his home. They took the girl with them.

He changed his story at least fifteen times. Despite this, prosecutors still decided to offer Walker a deal. He pled guilty to third degree murder and kidnapping in return for his testimony against the O'Brien brothers. His deal included an agreement for a maximum sentence of forty years.

On October 25, 2005, on the eve of the thirteenth anniversary of Howe's disappearance, both O'Brien brothers (then 33 and 39) were convicted on multiple charges, including murder, kidnapping, and involuntary deviate sexual intercourse (a charge similar in act and severity as rape).

They were acquitted of first-degree murder and rape, in part because for first-degree murder it must be proven that the crime was premeditated. The brothers were sentenced to life without parole.

Current Status:
When the DNA evidence came to light, the O'Brien's mother refused to believe it, saying what on earth would her sons want with a child.

James O'Brien claims his DNA was transferred to Howe's mouth and clothing as a result of an earlier event he had in the same bedroom with a woman. He claims that Walker was the one to actually molest Howe.

After Howe's kidnapping and death, Oil City became known as the town that banned Halloween. In 2008, three years after the O'Brien brothers were found guilty, 175 town citizens signed a petition started by a fifth-grader to allow nighttime trick or treating again.

The city agreed, and children once again were able to celebrate Halloween in Oil City.

Conclusion

I hope you found these stories to be as interesting to read as I did to research and write them. Learning of other's sorrows and triumphs helps each of us to be thankful for what and whom we have in our lives and also for the tireless efforts of the authorities that work each and every day to help keep us safe.

Many cities now have teams assigned to look at cold cases and see if more can be done now to solve them.

It also gives hope to the countless other friends and families still waiting out there for the person or persons who took their loved one away to be identified and brought to justice.

Dear Readers,

Thank you for purchasing this book. I enjoyed researching and writing about these cases and I hope you found them to be both interesting and engrossing.

If your friends and family would enjoy reading about this topic, please be sure to let them know about this book.

Again, thank you for your support and I look forward to writing more books of Murder, Scandals and Mayhem.

Regards,
Mike Riley

P.S. Remember to check out my other books and my new book...

*"**Innocence Executed:** True Stories of People Executed For Crimes They Did Not Commit"*
Coming Soon!

35422297R00063

Printed in Great Britain
by Amazon